PROTECTING THE HOMELAND FROM NUCLEAR AND RADIOLOGICAL THREATS

HEARING

BEFORE THE

SUBCOMMITTEE ON CYBERSECURITY, INFRASTRUCTURE PROTECTION, AND SECURITY TECHNOLOGIES

OF THE

COMMITTEE ON HOMELAND SECURITY HOUSE OF REPRESENTATIVES

ONE HUNDRED THIRTEENTH CONGRESS

SECOND SESSION

JULY 29, 2014

Serial No. 113–82

Printed for the use of the Committee on Homeland Security

Available via the World Wide Web: http://www.gpo.gov/fdsys/

U.S. GOVERNMENT PUBLISHING OFFICE

92–899 PDF   WASHINGTON : 2015

For sale by the Superintendent of Documents, U.S. Government Publishing Office
Internet: bookstore.gpo.gov   Phone: toll free (866) 512–1800; DC area (202) 512–1800
Fax: (202) 512–2104   Mail: Stop IDCC, Washington, DC 20402–0001

COMMITTEE ON HOMELAND SECURITY

MICHAEL T. McCAUL, Texas, *Chairman*

LAMAR SMITH, Texas
PETER T. KING, New York
MIKE ROGERS, Alabama
PAUL C. BROUN, Georgia
CANDICE S. MILLER, Michigan, *Vice Chair*
PATRICK MEEHAN, Pennsylvania
JEFF DUNCAN, South Carolina
TOM MARINO, Pennsylvania
JASON CHAFFETZ, Utah
STEVEN M. PALAZZO, Mississippi
LOU BARLETTA, Pennsylvania
RICHARD HUDSON, North Carolina
STEVE DAINES, Montana
SUSAN W. BROOKS, Indiana
SCOTT PERRY, Pennsylvania
MARK SANFORD, South Carolina
CURTIS CLAWSON, Florida

BENNIE G. THOMPSON, Mississippi
LORETTA SANCHEZ, California
SHEILA JACKSON LEE, Texas
YVETTE D. CLARKE, New York
BRIAN HIGGINS, New York
CEDRIC L. RICHMOND, Louisiana
WILLIAM R. KEATING, Massachusetts
RON BARBER, Arizona
DONDALD M. PAYNE, JR., New Jersey
BETO O'ROURKE, Texas
FILEMON VELA, Texas
ERIC SWALWELL, California
VACANCY
VACANCY

BRENDAN P. SHIELDS, *Staff Director*
JOAN O'HARA, *Acting Chief Counsel*
MICHAEL S. TWINCHEK, *Chief Clerk*
I. LANIER AVANT, *Minority Staff Director*

———

SUBCOMMITTEE ON CYBERSECURITY, INFRASTRUCTURE PROTECTION, AND SECURITY TECHNOLOGIES

PATRICK MEEHAN, Pennsylvania, *Chairman*

MIKE ROGERS, Alabama
TOM MARINO, Pennsylvania
JASON CHAFFETZ, Utah
STEVE DAINES, Montana
SCOTT PERRY, Pennsylvania, *Vice Chair*
MICHAEL T. McCAUL, Texas *(ex officio)*

YVETTE D. CLARKE, New York
WILLIAM R. KEATING, Massachusetts
FILEMON VELA, Texas
VACANCY
BENNIE G. THOMPSON, Mississippi *(ex officio)*

ALEX MANNING, *Subcommittee Staff Director*
DENNIS TERRY, *Subcommittee Clerk*

CONTENTS

————

Page

STATEMENTS

The Honorable Patrick Meehan, a Representative in Congress From the State of Pennsylvania, and Chairman, Subcommittee on Cybersecurity, Infrastructure Protection, and Security Technologies:
Oral Statement 1
Prepared Statement 3
The Honorable Yvette D. Clarke, a Representative in Congress From the State of New York, and Ranking Member, Subcommittee on Cybersecurity, Infrastructure Protection, and Security Technologies:
Oral Statement 3
Prepared Statement 5
The Honorable Bennie G. Thompson, a Representative in Congress From the State of Mississippi, and Ranking Member, Committee on Homeland Security:
Prepared Statement 6

WITNESSES

Ms. Huban A. Gowadia, Director, Domestic Nuclear Detection Office, Department of Homeland Security:
Oral Statement 7
Prepared Statement 9
Mr. David C. Trimble, Director, Natural Resources and Environment, U.S. Government Accountability Office:
Oral Statement 17
Prepared Statement 18

APPENDIX

Questions From Chairman Patrick Meehan For Huban Gowadia 39

PROTECTING THE HOMELAND FROM NUCLEAR AND RADIOLOGICAL THREATS

Tuesday, July 29, 2014

U.S. House of Representatives,
Committee on Homeland Security,
Subcommittee on Cybersecurity, Infrastructure
Protection, and Security Technologies,
Washington, DC.

The subcommittee met, pursuant to call, at 2:00 p.m., in Room 311, Cannon House Office Building, Hon. Patrick Meehan [Chairman of the subcommittee] presiding.

Present: Representatives Meehan and Clarke.

Mr. MEEHAN. The Committee on Homeland Security, Subcommittee on Cybersecurity, Infrastructure Protection, and Security Technologies will come to order.

The subcommittee is meeting today to examine the Department of Homeland Security's capabilities of protecting the homeland from nuclear or radiological attacks.

I now recognize myself for an opening statement.

The subcommittee meets today to examine a vitally important issue: Protecting the homeland from nuclear and radiological attack. I think if we just use those words alone, it identifies the seriousness and gravity of the issue. A nuclear or radiological attack, with its very scope, just so remarkably, sort-of, outperforms so many other forms of concern that we have.

So, given the alarming expansion of terrorist safe havens across the Middle East and North Africa, along with the increasing sophistication of these groups in organizing and planning attacks, it is imperative the Department of Homeland Security is properly prepared to detect and deter nuclear threats.

The Domestic Nuclear Detection Office, which we often refer to as DNDO, is the entity within the Department of Homeland Security responsible for preventing a nuclear attack and is the lead agency within the United States Government for coordinating efforts to detect and intercept radiological and nuclear devices that may find their way into the United States. DNDO coordinates these efforts through an interagency system and the collaborative framework that is known as the Global Nuclear Detection Architecture. DNDO is responsible for implementing that architecture domestically.

DNDO works with other Department of Homeland Security components, including Customs and Border Protection, as well as State and local law enforcement to provide these entities with the equipment and training needed to interdict radiological or nuclear mate-

(1)

rial before it can enter the United States. DNDO works closely with these components to install radiation portal monitors at ports of entry and supply officers with portable radiation monitors. Currently, 100 percent of all containerized cargo coming in is scanned at land and sea ports of entry into the United States.

DNDO also works with State and local law enforcement and first responders to strengthen nuclear detection capabilities in the interior. Through the Securing the Cities program, DNDO helps State, local, and Tribal governments design and implement detection and interdiction capabilities in high-density urban areas. The efforts in the New York City region have resulted in a robust detection architecture. Last year, DHS announced the STC program will be expanded to Los Angeles-Long Beach area, and they will select a third city in fiscal 2014.

While these achievements are significant, there is still work to be done to address the gaps in the nuclear detection architecture. The purpose of this hearing is to address those gaps and find how we can best assist DNDO and the Department to prevent a catastrophic nuclear event.

DNDO has had its share of struggles in the past—among them, failed acquisition plans and less-than-optimal working relationships with some of their other interagency components. In its report from 2013, the GAO—and it is important to note that this is why we have the GAO here, who has been taking a good arm's-length look at the activities—they noted these deficiencies and recommended approaches towards curing them. I will be interested in hearing some of that from our witness.

Since then, DNDO has successfully worked to implement GAO recommendations. I look forward to learning more about it, how the office has improved as a result of those efforts.

I pleased to welcome to this hearing our distinguished panel. Dr. Huban Gowadia is the director of the Domestic Nuclear Detection Office, and Dr. David Trimble is the director of Natural Resources and Environment at the U.S. Government Accountability Office.

DNDO plays a vital and specific role within the Homeland Security, and it is our responsibility to ensure that it has what it needs to protect and prevent a radiological or nuclear terrorist attack. I look forward to hearing from our witnesses on, and particularly Dr. Gowadia, how she envisions the future of DNDO.

I note also, while I talk about the catastrophic nuclear event that is potential in a world in which proliferation, particularly that which is going on in Iran and Iraq and other places in which there is perhaps not weapons themselves but certainly nuclear-grade material that can be used in other kinds of capacities, including dirty bombs and other things, we are talking about a broad spectrum of potential threats.

So we certainly are interested in the future and what DNDO and Congress can do and should do to help this office achieve its mission. So I am grateful for your presence here.

[The statement of Mr. Meehan follows:]

STATEMENT OF CHAIRMAN PATRICK MEEHAN

JULY 29, 2014

The subcommittee meets today to examine a vitally important issue: Protecting the homeland from nuclear and radiological attack. Given the alarming expansion of terrorist safe havens across the Middle East and Northern Africa, along with the increasing sophistication of these groups in organizing and planning attacks, it is imperative that the Department of Homeland Security is properly prepared to detect and deter nuclear threats.

The Domestic Nuclear Detection Office (DNDO) is the entity within the Department of Homeland Security responsible for preventing a nuclear attack, and is the lead agency within the U.S. Government for coordinating efforts to detect and intercept radiological and nuclear devices coming into the United States. DNDO coordinates these efforts through an interagency systems and collaborative framework known as the Global Nuclear Detection Architecture (GNDA), and DNDO is responsible for implementing the GNDA domestically.

DNDO works with other DHS components, including Customs and Border Protection, as well as State and local law enforcement, to provide these entities with the equipment and training needed to interdict radiological or nuclear material before it can enter the United States. DNDO works closely with these components to install radiation portal monitors at ports of entry and supply officers with portable radiation monitors. Currently 100% of all containerized cargo coming is scanned at land and sea ports of entry in the United States.

DNDO also works with State and local law enforcement and first responders to strengthen nuclear detection capabilities in the interior. Through the "Securing the Cities" program, DNDO helps State, local, and Tribal governments design and implement detection and interdiction capabilities in high-density urban areas. These efforts in New York City region have resulted in a robust detection architecture, and last year, DHS announced the STC program will be expanded to the Los Angeles-Long Beach area and will select a third city in fiscal year 2014.

While these achievements are significant, there is still work to be done to address gaps in the nuclear detection architecture. The purpose of this hearing is to address those gaps and find how we can best assist DNDO and the Department to prevent a catastrophic nuclear event.

DNDO has had its share of struggles in the past. Among them, failed acquisition plans, and less-than-optimal working relationships with some of its inter-agency counterparts. In its report from 2013, the Government Accountability Office (GAO) noted these deficiencies and recommended approaches toward curing them. Since then, DNDO has successfully worked to implement GAO's recommendations, and I look forward to learning more about how the Office has improved as a result of those efforts.

I am pleased to welcome to this hearing our distinguished panel of witnesses: Dr. Huban Gowadia, director of the Domestic Nuclear Detection Office, Dr. David Trimble, director, Natural Resources and Environment, U.S. Government Accountability Office. DNDO plays a vital and specific role within homeland security and it is our responsibility to ensure that it has what it needs to prevent a radiological or nuclear terrorist attack. I look forward to hearing from Dr. Gowadia how she envisions the future of DNDO, and what Congress can and should do to help the office achieve its mission.

Mr. MEEHAN. I now recognize the Ranking Minority Member of the subcommittee, the gentlelady from New York, Ms. Clarke, for any statement she may have.

Ms. CLARKE. I thank you, Mr. Chairman, for holding this hearing on the threats of radiological and nuclear smuggling that our country faces.

I want to thank our witnesses today, Dr. Gowadia, director of DNDO, and Mr. Trimble and the GAO team for agreeing to testify today.

The issues before us today include how to measure the balance between investment in near-term and long-term solutions for nuclear detection gaps and how we gauge the degree and efficiency of Federal agency coordination and especially the mechanisms that DNDO employs for setting agency investment priorities.

Today, we will hear about some of the achievements that the hard-working Federal and civilian employees of DNDO have accomplished to protect us. Other testimony today will help us understand the challenges that we experience in such a highly complex technological world preventing terrorists from acquiring, transporting, and using radiological materials as a weapon of terror.

If we are to think about reauthorizing this program, which I understand the Chairman is inclined to do, this subcommittee in its oversight responsibilities needs to possess ways to evaluate and measure the outcomes of DNDO's R&D activities, their resource requests, and their asset allocations.

I think it is safe to say that over the years this subcommittee has seen many examples of DNDO pushing for acquisition decisions well before some technologies had demonstrated that they could live up to the promises made. In my opinion, we must deal with this issue directly in any potential legislative language.

It will be paramount that DNDO policy and strategy be translated into operations, tactics, and implementation that meet the requirements of Department-wide needs and that this subcommittee be able to transparently see that process.

Furthermore, there are natural tensions among Federal agencies created by overlapping missions in the nuclear arena, especially in the field of nuclear detection. This fact of life does not make matters of policy and strategy easy to implement, nor outcomes easily measured.

Since 2009, after President Obama's administration, DNDO has made important changes and made especially good progress in nuclear forensics. I hope that our Congressional oversight efforts also have had a positive effect.

In 2010, the committee, under then-Chairman Thompson, wrote and combined S&T-DNDO authorizations, H.R. 4842, which set out the premise that research and development and operations and procurement are best left to separate organizations in order to avoid obvious and glaring conflicts of interest. While not all goals of that legislation were achieved, the message was clearly received by the administration.

What I hope we are going to hear today is: How can DNDO's mission be better-defined? Some claim there is still confusion as to whether the office is an end-to-end R&D procurement entity for all things nuclear and radiological. Is it a development entity, or an operational entity? Some still question whether there is an inherent conflict of interest when an office, agency, or program is both an R&D workshop and a procurement platform. I hope we can explore some of these questions today.

Let me finish with this thought. On the ground and every day, our nuclear deterrence effort as a Nation depends on motivated and vigilant officers across the globe supplied with the best equipment and intelligence we can give them. Officers working out of our Nation's ports of entry have an especially complex and difficult job. Thousands of decisions are made every day to clear a container or a personal or commercial vehicle for transit into the United States. Other cargo requires further inspection or even denial of entry or an interdiction action on a vehicle or person.

That is the hard, cold, repetitive, and everyday reality of our mission to prevent the kind of violent nuclear attack. However, this is part of the flow of commerce in the world's premier, leading trading market, the United States, and we are grateful for all of our dedicated women and men in the field who perform these vital tasks.

Mr. Chairman, I look forward to today's testimony, and I yield back.

[The statement of Ms. Clarke follows:]

STATEMENT OF RANKING MEMBER YVETTE D. CLARKE

JULY 29, 2014

Thank you, Mr. Chairman, for holding this hearing on the threats of radiological and nuclear smuggling our country faces. I want to thank our witnesses today, Dr. Gowadia, director of DNDO, and the GAO team for agreeing to testify today. The issues before us today include how to measure the balance between investment in near-term and long-term solutions for nuclear detection gaps, and how we gauge the degree and efficiency of Federal agency coordination, and especially the mechanisms that DNDO employs for setting agency investment priorities.

Today, we will hear about some of the achievements that the hard-working Federal and civilian employees of DNDO have accomplished to protect us. Other testimony today will help us understand the challenges that we experience in such a highly complex technological world—preventing terrorists from acquiring, transporting, and using radiological materials as a weapon of terror.

If we are to think about reauthorizing this program, which I understand the Chairman is inclined to do, this subcommittee, in its oversight responsibilities, needs to possess ways to evaluate and measure the outcomes of DNDO's R&D activities, their resource requests, and their asset allocations.

I think its safe to say that over the years, this subcommittee has seen many examples of DNDO pushing for acquisition decisions well before some technologies had demonstrated that they could live up to the promises made. In my opinion, we must deal with this issue directly in any potential legislative language.

It will be paramount that DNDO policy and strategy be translated into operations, tactics, and implementation that meet the requirements of Department-wide needs, and that this subcommittee be able to transparently see that process. Furthermore, there are natural tensions among Federal agencies created by overlapping missions in the nuclear arena, especially in the field of nuclear detection. This fact of life does not make matters of policy and strategy easy to implement, nor outcomes easily measured.

Since 2009, under President Obama's administration, DNDO has made important changes, and made especially good progress in nuclear forensics, and I hope that our Congressional oversight efforts also have had a positive effect. In 2010, the committee, under then-Chairman Thompson, wrote a combined S&T DNDO authorization, H.R. 4842, which set out the premise that research and development, and operations and procurement, are best left to separate organizations in order to avoid obvious and glaring conflicts of interest. While not all goals of that legislation were achieved, the message was clearly received by the administration.

What I hope we are going to hear today is, "How can DNDO's mission can be better defined"? Some claim there is still confusion as to whether the office is an end-to-end R&D procurement entity for all things nuclear/radiological . . . is it a development entity . . . or an operational entity?

Some still question whether there is an inherent conflict of interest when an office, agency, or program, is both an R&D workshop and a procurement platform. I hope we can explore some of these questions today.

Let me finish with this thought. On the ground, and every day, our nuclear deterrence effort as a Nation depends on motivated and vigilant officers across the globe, supplied with the best equipment and intelligence we can give them. Officers working at our Nation's ports of entry have an especially complex and difficult job. Thousands of decisions are made every day to clear a container or a personal or commercial vehicle for transit into the United States.

Other cargo requires further inspection—or even denial of entry—or an interdiction action on a vehicle or person. That is the hard, cold, repetitive, and everyday reality of our mission to prevent this kind of violent nuclear attack. However, this is part of the flow of commerce in the world's premier and largest trading market, the United States, and we are grateful for all of our dedicated men and women in the field who perform these vital tasks.

Mr. Chairman, I look forward to today's testimony, and I yield back.

Mr. MEEHAN. Let me thank the Ranking Member for her opening statement but also for her focus on the idea that our objective is to do, you know, effective oversight to assure that the resources are being appropriately focused. We look forward to the ability for the record to speak to those particular issues.

Other Members of the committee who may come in are reminded that opening statements may be submitted for the record.

[The statement of Ranking Member Thompson follows:]

STATEMENT OF RANKING MEMBER BENNIE G. THOMPSON

JULY 29, 2014

Thank you, Mr. Chairman, for holding this hearing on the Domestic Nuclear Detection Office, and the radiological and nuclear smuggling threats it faces. I want to thank the director of DNDO, and the GAO team for coming in to testify today.

We will hear testimony about some of the successes, and some of the challenges that still exist in preventing terrorists from acquiring, transporting, and using radiological materials as a potential weapon of terror.

We know that our nuclear detection strategy and equipment at the time of the 9/11 attacks was limited in its capability. Radiation detectors could sometimes detect radiation, but could not identify isotopes. We also found out that sensing equipment could reveal dense objects, but it would be almost impossible to pick out a small piece of Special Nuclear Material, or SNM. Today, as technologies have become more capable, they can fill more gaps in the current nuclear detection architecture.

But there's still a long way to go to fulfill the goals we set for DNDO, and many questions to ask. For example, are we making progress on remote detection that might offer a way to monitor chokepoints in the United States that terrorists might pass through transporting weapons?

And, we have identified other gaps, like the need for long-range sensors that can operate in isolated areas, and systems that can perform efficiently in highly-congested public maritime areas. These kinds of technologies and sensors do not come easily, or inexpensively.

But, we need to have systems under development that have the potential to reduce false positives, speed the flow of commerce, and reduce false negatives—all of which improve security. Over the years, Congress has appropriated billions of dollars to deploy systems to prevent nuclear smuggling, and to support R&D on advanced technologies.

What we hope for is that money Congress spends to achieve these refinements can make future technologies more effective, and create an R&D pipeline that is intended to generate a steady stream of new technologies and systems.

However, Congress must be sure that the money it spends for this technological pipeline is used wisely and efficiently, and that testing and certification of these cutting-edge tools are thoroughly evaluated and validated. Over the years, we have seen too many reports about detection technologies being deployed without proper testing, and without certification.

The development & procurement of sophisticated technologies is not a simple matter, but it is also not one that should be opaque and overly complicated for Congress to understand.

We know that DNDO has an important role across the Department, and that it has close relationships with DHS's front-line programs, and other Federal agencies, who depend on them for support and advice.

The challenge for this committee is how to evaluate how well DNDO meets the operational requirements for DHS programs, how it spends its money and prioritizes its R&D, and how it fulfills its responsibilities in coordinating the Global Nuclear Detection Architecture.

We will hear testimony from GAO today about the need for a clearer, and measurable picture of its goals, strategies, and procedures.

It is imperative that the new Secretary makes sure no more money is wasted on devices that cannot be properly evaluated, tested, and certified before being procured and placed into duty. Our country's safety depends on it.

Mr. Chairman, I look forward to today's testimony, and I yield back.

Mr. MEEHAN. We are pleased to have a distinguished panel of witnesses before us here today on this important topic.

First, Dr. Huban Gowadia is the director of the Domestic Nuclear Detection Office at the Department of Homeland Security. Under her leadership, DNDO develops nuclear detection capabilities, it measures detector system performance, it ensures effective response to detection alarms, it conducts transformational research and development, and it coordinates the improvement of technical nuclear forensics capabilities.

Before joining DNDO, Dr. Gowadia led DHS's Science and Technology countermeasures—the countermeasures testbeds and also worked as a checkpoint program manager at the Office of Security Technologies in the Transportation Security Administration.

We are joined, as well, by Mr. David Trimble, who serves as the director of the U.S. Government Accountability Office's Natural Resources and Environment Group. Mr. Trimble provided leadership and oversight on the United States and international nuclear security and clean-up issues.

Mr. Trimble joined GAO in 2009, and, previously, he worked at the Department of State's Political-Military Affairs Bureau as the director of the Office of Defense Trade Controls Compliance.

The witnesses' full written statements will appear in the record.

I know there are extensive written statements, but I want to give you the opportunity to focus on where you would like to go in your testimony, Dr. Gowadia. So we now recognize you for your 5 minutes to testify.

STATEMENT OF HUBAN A. GOWADIA, DIRECTOR, DOMESTIC NUCLEAR DETECTION OFFICE, DEPARTMENT OF HOMELAND SECURITY

Ms. GOWADIA. Thank you, Chairman. Good afternoon, Chairman Meehan and Ranking Member Clarke. Thank you for the opportunity to discuss the Domestic Nuclear Detection Office, or DNDO's, progress in protecting the homeland from nuclear and radiological threats.

I am honored to appear before you today to testify with my distinguished colleague, David Trimble. Your support and oversight and constructive feedback from the Government Accountability Office are critical to our improvement and continued success.

As you are aware, in 2005, DNDO was created within the Department of Homeland Security as an interagency office with a singular focus: Preventing nuclear terrorism. We do so through two missions, nuclear detection and nuclear forensics. Let me begin with the latter.

DNDO's National Technical Nuclear Forensics Center was established to provide centralized stewardship, planning, and integration for Federal nuclear forensics and attribution activities. At the time, the state of nuclear forensics capabilities were far from perfect, as emphasized in reports by the National Academy of Sciences, the GAO, and others. Since then, DNDO has advanced nuclear capabilities and improved collaborative National exercises by making them remarkably realistic. Focusing on what was then an in extremis National capability, DNDO has supported 19 new nuclear forensic scientists, and we are on track to add another 35 into the nuclear forensics field by 2018. I should say, a total of 35 by 2018.

So let me switch now to the detection mission. DNDO was established to coordinate the United States Government's radiological and nuclear detection capabilities through the construct of the Global Nuclear Detection Architecture. This is a framework for detecting, analyzing, and reporting on nuclear and other radioactive materials that are out of regulatory control. In accordance with the GAO's recommendations and along with our interagency partners, we developed the 2010 Global Nuclear Detection Architecture Strategic Plan. Recently, we updated it in 2014 based on feedback from the National Academy of Sciences.

DNDO is also mandated to conduct an aggressive program of transformational research and development. As a result of our efforts, several breakthrough sensing materials with enhanced detection characteristics have transitioned from the laboratory to commercially available products.

We also have a robust test and evaluation program. To date, DNDO has conducted more than 100 test campaigns and, with the National Institute of Standards and Technology, developed consensus standards for radiation detection equipment. Today, we have a total of 24 standards for homeland security applications.

To implement the domestic component of the Global Nuclear Detection Architecture, we have made much progress in equipping law enforcement officers and public safety officials with the necessary capabilities, information, and training. For instance, through the Securing the Cities program, we now have robust regional nuclear detection capabilities in major urban areas, including the New York City region and the L.A.-Long Beach region. Through collaborative interagency efforts, we have provided training to over 27,000 law enforcement personnel across the Nation. Annually, we conduct approximately 15 exercises to stress operator abilities to detect illicit nuclear and other radioactive material.

In our role as the Department lead for acquiring radiation assistance, we bring a disciplined approach to procurement. DNDO's efforts have ensured that all Coast Guard boarding parties carry radiation detection equipment. All incoming general aviation aircraft are met by Customs and Border Protection Officers with detectors. One hundred percent of conveyances entering our Nation at land ports of entry are scanned for radiological and nuclear material, and almost 100 percent of maritime cargo is similarly scanned at our seaports of entry. Finally, the Transportation Security Administration's Visible Intermodal Prevention and Response teams are also equipped with radiation detectors.

To ensure that we do not repeat the same issues that led to the cancellation of the Advanced Spectroscopic Portal Program, DNDO significantly improved acquisition management governance, policy, and processes. We have implemented a disciplined solution development process, establishing a common lexicon with consistent practices and deliberately and continually involving operational partners. As a result, we have increased efficiencies, promoted programmatic and budgetary transparency, and bolstered accountability for all our programs.

Looking forward, we will continue to build and sustain critical partnerships across the nuclear security enterprise. We will use an effective risk-informed approach to guide our efforts. We will strive to leverage technical breakthroughs to enhance our National nuclear detection and forensics capabilities. Importantly, we will continue to improve the discipline in procuring and deploying systems to meet the needs of our operational partners.

Thank you again for this opportunity, and I look forward to your questions.

[The prepared statement of Ms. Gowadia follows:]

PREPARED STATEMENT OF HUBAN A. GOWADIA

JULY 29, 2014

Chairman Meehan, Ranking Member Clarke, and distinguished Members of the subcommittee, thank you for the opportunity to appear before you today. I appreciate your interest in the advancements the Department of Homeland Security's (DHS) Domestic Nuclear Detection Office (DNDO) has made in preventing nuclear terrorism. I am honored to testify with my distinguished colleagues from the Government Accountability Office and the National Academy of Sciences. Your support and oversight, and their constructive assessments and feedback, are critical to our improvement and continued success.

Nuclear terrorism remains a serious risk because of its potential consequences. As President Obama stated in his speech at South Korea's Hankuk University in March 2012, "We know that just the smallest amount of plutonium—about the size of an apple—could kill hundreds of thousands and spark a global crisis. The danger of nuclear terrorism remains one of the greatest threats to global security." To address this risk, DNDO was established as a unique interagency organization with a singular focus on preventing nuclear terrorism. Reducing the risk of nuclear terrorism is a whole-of-Government challenge, and DNDO works with Federal, State, local, Tribal, territorial, and international partners as well as those in the private sector, academia, and the National laboratories to fulfill its mission.

AUTHORITIES

Recognizing the threat posed by nuclear and other radioactive materials, DNDO was created by National Security Presidential Directive (NSPD)–43 and Homeland Security Presidential Directive (HSPD)–14 and subsequently codified by Title V of the Security and Accountability For Every (SAFE) Port Act (Pub. L. No. 109–347), which amended the Homeland Security Act of 2002. Pursuant to section 1902 of the Homeland Security Act, DNDO is required to develop, with the approval of the Secretary and in coordination with the Departments of Energy, State, Defense, and Justice, an enhanced global nuclear detection architecture, and is responsible for implementing the domestic portion. The architecture serves as a framework for detecting (through technical and non-technical means), analyzing, and reporting on nuclear and other radioactive materials that are out of regulatory control. Non-technical detection refers to an alert caused by law enforcement or intelligence efforts and collected by GNDA partners under their statutory authorities and consistent with National policy. DNDO is also charged to enhance and coordinate the nuclear detection efforts of Federal, State, local, and Tribal governments and the private sector to ensure a managed, coordinated response. To accomplish this, DNDO leads programs to develop nuclear detection and forensics capabilities, measure detector system performance, ensure effective response to detection alarms, and conduct transformational research and development for advanced detection technologies.

In 2006, DNDO's National Technical Nuclear Forensics Center was established by NSPD–17/HSPD–4 and later authorized by the 2010 Nuclear Forensics and Attribution Act (Pub. L. No. 111–140). The Center was given responsibilities to provide centralized stewardship, planning, and integration for all Federal nuclear forensics and attribution activities. The act also established DNDO's National Nuclear Forensics Expertise Development program and required DNDO to lead the development and implementation of the National Strategic Five-Year Plan for Improving the Nuclear Forensics and Attribution Capabilities of the United States.

These authorities have directed our focus in preventing nuclear terrorism through the enhancement of nuclear detection and technical forensics capabilities. In both instances, we rely on the critical triad of intelligence, law enforcement, and technology. Thus, to maximize the Nation's ability to detect and interdict a threat, it is imperative that we apply detection technologies in operations that are driven by intelligence indicators, and place them in the hands of well-trained law enforcement and public safety officials. Similarly, to enhance attribution capabilities, the U.S. Government (USG) must ensure that information from law enforcement, intelligence, and technical nuclear forensics is fused to identify the origin of the material or device and the perpetrators.

While we have made significant improvements in both detection and forensics over the years, the threat of nuclear terrorism persists, and requires constant vigilance.

DEVELOPING THE GLOBAL NUCLEAR DETECTION ARCHITECTURE

As recognized by the Government Accountability Office in past testimonies, DNDO has made progress in its strategic planning efforts. In December 2010, DNDO issued the first-ever Global Nuclear Detection Architecture Strategic Plan to guide the development and implementation of USG detection programs, activities, and capabilities. In April 2012, the Secretary issued a DHS Global Nuclear Detection Architecture Implementation Plan, which identified priorities, necessary capabilities, and monitoring mechanisms to assess progress. DNDO has worked with interagency partners to update the Global Nuclear Detection Architecture Strategic Plan. The 2014 Strategic Plan presents an updated definition and vision for the global nuclear detection architecture, as well as a mission, goals, and objectives for interagency efforts to detect, analyze, and report on nuclear or other radioactive materials that are out of regulatory control.

The global nuclear detection architecture is a multi-faceted, layered, defense-in-depth framework, with the objective of making the illicit acquisition, fabrication, and transport of a nuclear or radiological device, material, or components prohibitively difficult. DNDO also relies on a well-conceived arrangement of fixed and mobile radiological and nuclear technical detection capabilities to present terrorists with many obstacles to a successful attack, greatly increasing costs, difficulty, and risk, and thereby deterring them.

To develop such a multi-faceted global nuclear detection architecture, DNDO continually assesses current and planned capabilities against the evolving radiological and nuclear threat. DNDO uses rigorous risk assessments as one means to do so. Since 2007, and as directed by HSPD–18 (Medical Countermeasures Against Weapons of Mass Destruction), DNDO has collaborated with the DHS Science & Technology Directorate (S&T) to produce the Integrated Chemical, Biological, Radiological, and Nuclear Terrorism Risk Assessment. DNDO leads the biennial radiological and nuclear terrorism risk assessment, which is then combined with similar biological and chemical risk assessments. To better address the evolving threat, DNDO has improved the threat models in this risk assessment by adding an adaptive adversary model and is working with Department of Energy (DOE) National Laboratories to enhance improvised nuclear device models. DNDO has also supported DHS risk assessments such as the Strategic National Risk Assessment and the Homeland Security National Risk Characterization. These risk assessments, coupled with requirements from our operational partners, inform DNDO resource allocations.

While USG efforts and programs are critical, developing a global nuclear detection architecture relies largely on the decisions of sovereign foreign partners to develop and enhance their own National and regional detection programs. DNDO contributes to interagency efforts led by the Department of State by laying the groundwork to assist partner nations in developing defense-in-depth approaches to detecting illicitly-trafficked nuclear or other radioactive materials. DOE's National Nuclear Security Administration's (NNSA) Second Line of Defense program is an essential component of this defense-in-depth approach. This program helps strengthen the global nuclear detection architecture by installing and supporting the installation of fixed and mobile radiation detection equipment at high-priority locations outside the United States. DNDO has worked closely with NNSA on training initiatives associated with building and sustaining foreign partners' radiation detection capabilities. DNDO has assisted in the development of guidelines and best practices through the Global Initiative to Combat Nuclear Terrorism and the International Atomic Energy Agency (IAEA) to outline the key characteristics of an effective architecture. To date, IAEA has used these guidelines and best practices in regional training courses to help more than 20 nations initiate planning of national-level detection architectures, with over 50 national-level planners trained in architecture development. Just two weeks ago (July 14–18, 2014), DNDO helped the IAEA expand its Nuclear Security Detection Architecture awareness course during a train-the-trainer session to further develop the international instructor pool. By the end of this calendar year, the IAEA will have successfully implemented seven regional awareness courses in English, French, and Spanish. This strategic partnership will continue to serve as a "force multiplier" for USG nuclear security efforts for years to come.

CONDUCTING TRANSFORMATIONAL RESEARCH AND DEVELOPING SYSTEMS

DNDO is also responsible for conducting an aggressive, evolutionary, and transformational program of research and development to generate and improve technologies to technically detect nuclear and radioactive materials. DNDO's transformational research and development efforts seek to achieve dramatic advancements in technologies to enhance our National detection and forensics capabilities. These developments may also reduce the cost and operational burden of using advanced technology in the field to maintain an enhanced level of protection. Annually, DNDO updates its research and development strategy based on prevailing risk, advancements in technology, and the availability of funding.

Although significant progress has been made in addressing the gaps and needs of the global nuclear detection architecture and nuclear forensics, several challenges remain that require sustained investment. DNDO's technical challenges include the need for systems that:

- Are cost-effective with sufficient technical performance to ensure wide-spread deployment;
- Can detect special nuclear material, even when heavily shielded;
- Facilitate enhanced wide-area searches in a variety of scenarios, to include urban and highly cluttered environments;
- Can be used to monitor traffic in challenging pathways, such as between ports of entry along our land and sea borders; and
- Support the forensics determination of origin and process history of seized material.

DNDO has and will continue to advance fundamental knowledge in nuclear detection and forensics through a sustained long-term investment in our Exploratory Research program and Academic Research Initiative. These efforts directly address the aforementioned challenges through basic and early-applied research to feed more mature research and development projects such as DNDO's Advanced Technology Demonstrations.

Equally important, the Academic Research Initiative is building the capabilities of universities to develop next generation scientists and engineers in areas such as advanced materials, nuclear engineering, radiochemistry, and deterrence theory. Since its inception, 57 grants have been awarded to more than 42 academic institutions across the country. In 2013 alone, the Academic Research Initiative directly supported 140 students, published 108 papers, and conducted 180 conference presentations. And, we are beginning to see these projects move up the technology pipeline. Just this year, a new room temperature thallium-based semiconductor detector transferred from Northwestern University to our Exploratory Research program. Nuclear resonance cross-sections measured at Duke University are being used in our shielded special nuclear material detection projects and background radiation measurements performed by University of California at Berkeley are being used in support of operational programs across the interagency.

Several DNDO-sponsored research efforts have also led to new commercial products that provide enhanced operational capabilities to Federal, State, and local law enforcement and public safety personnel. Even before a Helium–3 shortage was identified, DNDO teamed with the Defense Threat Reduction Agency to explore options for better, more cost-effective alternatives for neutron detection (Helium–3 is a gas that is widely used to detect neutrons that are emitted by certain nuclear and other radioactive materials. Helium–3 results from the radioactive decay of tritium. As the need for tritium for nuclear weapons decreased, so too did the availability of Helium–3.) For portal systems, which require the largest quantities of this gas, DNDO worked with industry and is now deploying alternative detection technologies that do not require Helium–3. This enables the country to devote the scarce supplies of Helium–3 to those applications where no substitutes are possible. We are also testing alternative systems for use in mobile, backpack, and hand-held radiation detectors, several of which have already shown performance superior to the current-generation systems. Importantly, due to a collaborative USG-wide effort to address the shortfall, our USG strategic reserve of Helium–3 has increased by 70% since 2009.

Other recent DNDO technological successes that transitioned from laboratories to commercially-available products include:

- Advanced radiation-sensing materials such as Cesium Lithium Yttrium Chloride, Strontium Iodide, and Stilbene, which have enhanced detection characteristics and can be used to build more capable systems featuring simplified electronics, low power requirements, and greater reliability;
- New electronics and advanced algorithms that support networked radiation detection for improved wide-area search capabilities;
- Compact dual-energy X-ray generators with improved density discrimination and higher shielding penetration that have been integrated into commercially available mobile radiography systems; and
- Software to automatically detect special nuclear material and shielding material in radiography images.

DNDO continues to develop breakthrough technologies that increase performance and reduce the operational burdens of our front-line operators. DNDO continues to work closely with other DHS components to improve their mission performance.

We are collaborating with U.S. Customs and Border Protection's (CBP) Laboratories and Scientific Services to use machine learning to greatly reduce the number of nuisance alarms in radiation portal monitors; working with the Massachusetts Port Authority, DHS S&T, and the United Kingdom Home Office to develop and evaluate the next generation non-intrusive inspection imaging equipment; and continuing to jointly evaluate parameter-setting modifications to reduce the number of alarms from naturally-occurring radioactive material. In fact, after a rigorous program of laboratory tests, modeling and simulation, field trials, and successful pilots at two ports of entry, CBP will deploy a new technique to the 26 largest seaports by the end of 2014. It is anticipated that this effort will reduce wait times and yield operational efficiencies.

In addition to CBP, DNDO worked closely with the U.S. Coast Guard (USCG), the Transportation Security Administration (TSA), and State and local partners to identify key operational requirements for the design of next-generation radioisotope identification devices that can be used by law enforcement officers and technical experts during routine operations to identify radioactive materials. Based on the enhanced detection material lanthanum bromide and improved algorithms, this new hand-held technology is easy-to-use, lightweight, and more reliable and, because it contains built-in calibration and diagnostics, has a much lower annual maintenance cost. The new system is receiving very positive reviews from operators in the field.

CHARACTERIZING SYSTEM PERFORMANCE

DNDO's technology efforts are coupled with a rigorous test and evaluation program. Over the years, DNDO's test program has grown and matured. To date, we have conducted more than 100 test and evaluation campaigns at more than 40 laboratory and operational venues, and evaluated systems including pagers, handhelds, portals, backpacks, and vehicle-, boat-, aircraft,- and spreader bar-mounted detectors, as well as next-generation radiography technologies. To ensure the equipment is evaluated in the manner in which it will be used, these test campaigns are always planned and executed with operational users. In addition, we include interagency partners and use peer-reviewed processes. The results from DNDO's test campaigns have informed Federal, State, local, and Tribal partners on the technical and operational performance of detection systems, allowing them to select the most suitable equipment and implement the most effective concepts of operation.

DNDO leads the development of technical capability standards, and in collaboration with the National Institute of Standards and Technology, also supports the development, publication, and adoption of National consensus standards for radiation detection equipment. A total of 24 standards, including 11 U.S. standards with the American National Standards Institute, 10 international standards with the International Electrotechnical Commission, and 3 technical capability standards now exist for homeland security applications. We have assessed commercially available detection systems against National and international standards and in various operational scenarios. Notably, we recently completed the Illicit Trafficking Radiation Assessment program, a collaboration with the European Commission's Joint Research Center and the IAEA to evaluate nearly 80 instruments against consensus standards. The results enabled our stakeholders to compare the performance of commercially available radiation detection equipment and provided manufacturers with constructive feedback on their products.

IMPLEMENTING THE DOMESTIC COMPONENT OF THE GLOBAL NUCLEAR DETECTION ARCHITECTURE

DNDO is instrumental in implementing the domestic component of the global nuclear detection architecture. In conjunction with Federal, State, local, Tribal, and territorial operational partners, DNDO applies a disciplined approach to procure small- and large-scale radiation detection and/or identification systems and deploy them at ports of entry, along our land and maritime borders, and in the interior of the United States. In addition, as part of DHS's Strategic Sourcing efforts, DNDO is the Department's commodity manager for hand-held radiological and nuclear detection equipment. This enables us to take advantage of technical advancements and achieve cost savings by leveraging the volume demand of Department-wide and other Federal users.

DNDO's collaborative system acquisition efforts have ensured that all USCG boarding parties carry radiation detection equipment; all in-coming general aviation flights are met by CBP Officers with radiation detectors; 100% of conveyances entering our Nation at land ports of entry are scanned for nuclear and other radioactive materials; almost 100% of maritime cargo is similarly scanned at our sea ports of entry; and the TSA's Visible Intermodal Prevention and Response teams are equipped with radiation detectors. Our partnership with CBP was leveraged during the recovery efforts from Hurricane Sandy. DNDO was able to replace 39 radiological detector panels and nine operator booths within 2 weeks of the storm, thereby supporting the quick resumption of port operations at A.P. Moller, Maher, Port Newark Container, New York Container, Global, and Red Hook terminals in New York and New Jersey. While technology acquisition and deployments are critical, we must also ensure that the training, exercise, and cross-jurisdictional protocols integral to mission success are adopted and sustained by operational partners. As such, DNDO provides program assistance services to Federal, State, local, Tribal, and territorial stakeholders who are developing or enhancing radiological and nuclear detection capabilities. This support includes assistance in developing and integrating local or regional programs into the global nuclear detection architecture, guiding the development of concepts of operations and standard operating procedures, and developing training and exercise products to ingrain those procedures into day-to-day activities.

DNDO has made considerable progress in enhancing National radiation detection capabilities by:

- Engaging with 29 States to raise awareness and begin developing formal radiological and nuclear detection programs. By the end of fiscal year 2015, DNDO plans to expand its efforts to all 50 States.
- Developing an enduring partnership with State and local jurisdictions, through the Securing the Cities program, resulting in a robust regional nuclear detection program in the New York City/Jersey City/Newark region. Based on lessons learned in this implementation, DNDO expanded the Securing the Cities program in fiscal year 2013 to the Los Angeles/Long Beach area and will select a third region later this fiscal year.
- Supporting domestic maritime capability development by working with regional Area Maritime Security Committees to develop operational procedures, training, and exercises to reinforce their Area Maritime Security Plans and address the small vessel threat.
- Deploying Mobile Detection Deployment Units to provide radiation detection and communications equipment for Federal, State, and local agencies to augment their capabilities during special events or in response to elevated threat conditions. To date, these units have been deployed over 150 times.

DNDO provides training products and support to develop, enhance, and expand radiological and nuclear detection capabilities. In partnership with the Federal Emergency Management Agency (FEMA) the Federal Law Enforcement Training Center, DOE, and the Department of Justice (DOJ), DNDO develops and implements protocols and training standards for the effective use of radiation detection equipment and associated alarm reporting and resolution processes. DNDO has developed 42 separate courses in support of emerging detection technologies and operational environments to support our Federal, State, and local stakeholders. Since 2005, more than 27,000 law enforcement and public safety personnel from 35 States have participated in DNDO-supported radiological and nuclear detection training.

DNDO also assists State and local partners in developing, designing, and conducting exercises that are compliant with the Homeland Security Exercise and Evaluation program methodology. The exercises provide valuable hands-on experience for personnel performing radiological and nuclear detection operations and assist decision makers in integrating the detection mission into their daily operations. To date, DNDO has conducted exercises with 21 States and annually supports up to 15–20 exercises. DNDO continues to develop and apply standardized and customizable exercise templates and guidelines evaluating the implementation and performance of Federal, State, and local radiological and nuclear detection programs while fostering the exchange of ideas and best practices amongst State and local partners.

DNDO fields a unique Red Team to objectively assess the operational effectiveness and performance of DNDO programs and deployed radiological and nuclear detection capabilities at the Federal, State, and local levels. Our Red Team works across the inter-agency employing an all-of-Government approach to collectively improving our National capabilities. At the Federal level we partner with the Departments of Energy, Defense, and Justice; within DHS with CBP, FEMA, TSA, USCG, and U.S. Secret Service; and with a myriad of State and local agencies across the United States. The Red Team evaluates deployed systems and operations and their associated tactics, techniques, and procedures, in as-close-to-realistic environments as possible. As covert and overt assessments are generally the only opportunity for operators of radiological and nuclear detection systems to gain experience detecting uncommon nuclear sources, these operations provide valuable feedback on the performance of tactics, techniques, and procedures. This feedback enables operators to improve their concepts of operation and readiness. For the past 5 years, DNDO's Red Team has averaged more than 25 overt and covert assessments per year.

DNDO is responsible for enhancing and coordinating the nuclear detection efforts of Federal, State, local, and Tribal governments and the private sector to ensure a managed, coordinated response. We also coordinate across the interagency to establish protocols and procedures to ensure that the technical detection of unauthorized nuclear explosive devices, fissile material, or other active radioactive material is promptly reported to the Secretaries of Homeland Security, Defense, and Energy, the Attorney General, and others as appropriate for action by law enforcement, military, emergency response, or other authorities.

DNDO's Joint Analysis Center is essential in enhancing situational awareness, as well as providing technical support and informational products, to Federal, State, and local partners. The Joint Analysis Center employs a secure web-based dashboard to collaborate with mission partners and uses a geographic information system to show detection information, detectors, situational awareness reports, and other overlays in a geospatial viewer. Using the Joint Analysis Center Collaborative Information System, DNDO facilitates nuclear alarm adjudication and the consolidation and sharing of information and databases. This system provides our State and local partners with the ability to manage, document, and execute a radiological and nuclear detection program. This includes the ability to electronically maintain training, certification, and Memoranda of Understanding and Memoranda of Agreement between jurisdictions. The system also consolidates and maintains a database of detector equipment and Nuclear Regulatory Commission State licensees. Through this information system, we connect to the Triage system, maintained by DOE's NNSA, to enable a seamless transition when National-level adjudication assistance is required. To increase awareness of lost and stolen sources and other relevant information, DNDO's Joint Analysis Center publishes weekly information bulletins, summarizing relevant news articles and providing useful facts about radioactive materials.

In addition to direct interaction with individual States and law enforcement agencies, DNDO hosts biennial State and Local Stakeholder Working Group meetings and annual Executive Steering Council meetings with law enforcement and other supervisory personnel to exchange best practices and to obtain feedback on DNDO's initiatives. The State and Local Stakeholder Working Group provides a forum for DNDO to meet with our stakeholders to discuss their current activities, lessons learned, and planned detection initiatives. This forum also provides State and local leaders an opportunity to convey their perspective on mission needs and radiation detection requirements, so that DNDO can develop the necessary products and services to support their efforts. The Executive Steering Council provides policy coordination and implementation between DNDO and senior-level State and local leaders regarding radiation detection programs, and serves as a mechanism to solicit input from senior leaders on their successes, evolving requirements, and challenges, as well as for DNDO to apprise them of on-going efforts to support their jurisdictions. Both the Stakeholder Working Group and the Executive Steering Council have been received favorably and continue to reinforce the relationship between DNDO and key stakeholders.

ACQUISITION PROCESS IMPROVEMENTS

Initiated in 2004 and canceled in 2011, the Advanced Spectroscopic Portal program was started with the goal of improving the performance of the current radiation detection system that is deployed to our seaports and land border crossings. To ensure we did not repeat the same issues that led to the cancellation of the program, including close end-user collaboration, DNDO and CBP completed a Lessons Learned/Post-Implementation Review and identified 32 lessons learned, including significant findings in acquisition management. DNDO will share these observations with the new DHS Joint Requirements Council to ensure maximum benefit is achieved from these past difficulties. Based in part on these lessons learned, DNDO has significantly bolstered acquisition management policy and strengthened its implementation via robust and disciplined governance and program management processes. In doing so, we ensure programs are selected based on sound business cases and are effectively managed, resulting in an efficient and effective use of DNDO's appropriated funds.

To enhance mission delivery and improve investment management, DNDO designed the Solution Development Process. Aligned with DHS Acquisition Management Directive 102–01, the Solution Development Process institutes an integrated governance approach to program and project oversight throughout the systems engineering life cycle. The process brings all programs and projects under governance—establishing a shared language, with common practices to increase efficiencies, promote programmatic and budgetary transparency, and bolster accountability. It aligns with DHS enterprise architecture, acquisition management, and capital planning and investment processes. Further, the framework guides management, through the Governance Review Board, and Integrated Product Teams in the delivery of new solution concepts to end-users and stakeholders, while maintaining a focus on DNDO's mission, goals, and objectives. As a critical component of the process, it includes active involvement of operational partners, who serve as Lead Business Authorities, and requires rigorous technical reviews at each programmatic stage. In adhering to the process, DNDO ensures current and future programs are appropriately structured and have the necessary oversight for success. DNDO will continue to incorporate lessons learned and process improvements as the process matures, sharing them throughout DHS to strengthen Departmental Unity of Effort—one of the Secretary's top priorities.

Recognizing the important contributions and innovations of private industry, National laboratories, and academia, DNDO has evolved its acquisition focus from one that is predominantly fueled by a Government-funded, Government-managed development process to one that relies upon industry-led development. As such, DNDO technology development programs now proceed with a "commercial first" approach; engaging first with the private sector for solutions and only moving to a Government-sponsored and -managed development effort if necessary. This approach leverages industry-led innovation, takes advantage of industry's innate flexibility and ability to rapidly improve technologies, and reduces Government-funded development efforts. In some cases, shifting to commercial-based acquisitions will reduce the total time to test, acquire, and field technology.

FORENSICS CAPABILITIES

In the event of an act of nuclear terrorism or interdiction there will be enormous pressure for rapid, accurate attribution. The resulting USG response will have to be supported by sound scientific evidence supporting the determination of who was responsible, for which the bar will be set very high by our stakeholders and allies. Nuclear forensics—as the technical pillar of attribution—will support leadership decisions. DNDO's National Technical Nuclear Forensics Center focuses on continuously evaluating and improving the nuclear forensic capabilities with specific responsibilities to:
- Improve the readiness of the overarching USG nuclear forensic capabilities, from pre- to post-detonation, through centralized stewardship, planning, assessment, gap analysis, exercises, improvement, and integration;
- Advance the technical capabilities of the USG to perform forensic analyses on pre-detonation nuclear and other radioactive materials; and
- Build and sustain an expertise pipeline for nuclear forensic scientists.

Operational readiness has improved markedly in recent years. DNDO has led the way in integrating the nuclear forensics community through the alignment of program capabilities, coordination of research and development and operational activities, and accelerated capability development through synchronized interagency investments. The interagency uses two primary DNDO-led mechanisms, the Nuclear Forensics Executive Council and Steering Committee, to facilitate consistent coordination across the USG. DNDO is also leading the interagency effort to update the National Strategic Five-Year Plan for Improving the Nuclear Forensics and Attribution Capabilities of the United States and to synchronize resources among partner agencies through an established Budget Crosscut. Requirements are now regularly identified and developed by the Nuclear Forensics Requirements Center, co-chaired by DNDO and the FBI.

Since the Nuclear Security Summit in 2010, international partnerships in nuclear forensics have greatly expanded, resulting in stronger National and international capabilities. DNDO provides subject-matter expertise to numerous initiatives, including multinational nuclear forensics table-top exercises and documentation, to enhance understanding among policy makers, law enforcement officials, and scientists, and to encourage and assist other nations in developing their National capabilities.

Forensics exercises have become realistic and complex, with intensive multi-agency planning among the FBI, DOE, Army, Air Force, and DNDO. Many of the exercises now include State and local law enforcement. Other exercises have involved the intelligence community, in order to plan and synchronize the fusion of intelligence, law enforcement and technical forensics information, leading to a more efficient and effective attribution process.

Nuclear forensics capabilities for analysis of nuclear and other radioactive materials have steadily advanced. DNDO's efforts are focused on continually improving the accuracy, precision, and timeliness of material characterization information, and linking that information to the process and place of that material's origin. To date, DNDO has developed seven radiological and nuclear certified reference materials, which are forensically-relevant calibration standards used by the National laboratories to improve confidence in analytical conclusions. Additionally, DNDO has developed the first-ever laboratory-scale uranium processing capability that allows us to determine forensic signatures associated with specific variations in uranium manufacturing processes. This capability enables us to determine forensics signatures without having direct access to samples from foreign fuel cycles. We are now beginning development of a similar plutonium processing capability. Further, in cooperation with DOE and the Department of Defense, DNDO has developed and installed a nuclear forensics data evaluation capability at Sandia National Laboratories that enables forensic analysts to develop and test data analysis tools and evaluate large sets of data in order to identify distinguishing characteristics of specific nuclear materials. Together with the remainder of our portfolio, these projects are significantly improving the National ability to trace nuclear materials back to their source.

DNDO's efforts to restore the expertise pipeline have also shown substantial success to date. The Congressionally-mandated National Nuclear Forensics Expertise Development program is a comprehensive effort to grow and sustain the scientific expertise required to execute the National technical nuclear forensics mission. Launched in 2008, this effort is a key component in assuring a robust and enduring nuclear forensics capability and its contribution to the Nation's efforts at preventing nuclear terrorism. In close partnership with eight National Laboratories, the program has provided support to more than 300 students and faculty and 23 universities. In 2008, DNDO commissioned an independent expert panel, the Nuclear Forensics Science Panel Education Sub-Panel, to examine the deficiencies in the nuclear forensics expertise pipeline and make recommendations to address them. We are steadily progressing toward the initial milestone, as established by the Science Panel's recommendation, of adding 35 new Ph.D. scientists into the nuclear forensics field by 2018 to replace anticipated attrition or retirements from the DOE National Laboratories. Nineteen new nuclear forensics scientists have come through the National Nuclear Forensics Expertise Development program and been hired since the program's inception.

CLOSING

While DNDO has made considerable progress since it was established in 2005, much remains to be done. It will be a challenge to remain one step ahead of the adversary—particularly one that is intelligent and adaptable. We must ensure our efforts are robust so that the obstacles terrorists face are many. DNDO's detection and forensics programs, in concert with those of our partners and stakeholders, are foundational elements in creating these impediments. Together, we can build upon DNDO's integrated approach to architecture planning, testing, and assessments, research and development, operational support, and nuclear forensics to strengthen the Nation's capabilities to detect and interdict the nuclear threat and to hold those responsible accountable for their actions. We remain committed to this challenge and we deeply appreciate this subcommittee's sustained interest and support in these shared goals to secure the homeland.

Thank you again for this opportunity, I would be happy to answer any questions from the committee.

Mr. MEEHAN. Thank you, Doctor.

The Chairman now recognizes the gentleman from the GAO, Mr. Trimble.

STATEMENT OF DAVID C. TRIMBLE, DIRECTOR, NATURAL RE-SOURCES AND ENVIRONMENT, U.S. GOVERNMENT ACCOUNT-ABILITY OFFICE

Mr. TRIMBLE. Chairman Meehan, Ranking Member Clarke, and Members of the committee—when they arrive—my testimony today discusses GAO's past work related to DNDO and provides preliminary observations from our on-going work for this subcommittee on management and coordination of research and development at DNDO.

DNDO's mission is critical to the Nation's capability to deter a radiological or nuclear attack within the United States. DNDO carries out this mission by coordinating the Global Nuclear Detection Architecture, developing and deploying radiation detection technology along our borders, and funding research and development of radiation and nuclear detection technology.

Since 2006, we have reported on progress and challenges in DNDO's efforts to develop plans for the GNDA and deploy radiation detection technology. We are pleased to report that DNDO has taken actions to respond to the majority of our recommendations in this area, including developing strategic and implementation plans for this effort.

In 2012, we reported on how DHS coordinates research and development across the agency, including at DNDO. We found that DHS did not have a Department-wide policy defining R&D or guidance directing components on how to report R&D investments, making it difficult for DHS to track and coordinate these efforts to prevent unnecessary duplication.

In 2013, we reviewed the extent to which DHS coordinates its border and maritime R&D efforts and found that work remained to be done to ensure these investments are directed towards the highest-priority needs.

One of the significant findings from our past work on DNDO's efforts to acquire and deploy radiation detection equipment was inadequate communication. We specifically found that DNDO sought to acquire an advanced system for detecting nuclear materials without understanding that the system would not fit in the inspection lanes operated by CBP. DNDO cancelled the system and limited any further work to research and development. This history highlights the importance of effective coordination in the early research and development phases of a system.

Our on-going work for this subcommittee examines management and coordination issues within the research directorate at DNDO. DNDO established this directorate, known as TAR, to identify, explore, and develop scientific and technological approaches that address gaps in the GNDA, improve the performance of existing detectors, and increase the efficiency of detection technology for the end-users who will operate it.

Regarding the TAR Directorate's efforts to manage R&D investments, our preliminary observations are that DNDO has taken steps to manage R&D and assess project outcomes, but the directorate may not be able to demonstrate how agency investments align with critical mission needs.

Critical mission needs are identified based on an analysis of gaps in the GNDA. However, TAR Directorate officials say they do not have systematic approach for evaluating its overall R&D program against the gaps in the GNDA. TAR Directorate officials told us they understand how projects are intended to make progress on those gaps but acknowledge that the only documentation on this linkage are large technical project deliverables.

As a result, the TAR Directorate may not be able to demonstrate to key stakeholders, including oversight organizations and potential users of new technologies, that its R&D investments are aligned with critical mission needs.

Regarding the TAR Directorate's efforts to coordinate R&D, our preliminary analysis shows that not all of DNDO's end-users are satisfied with the TAR Directorate's level of communications. In essence, the TAR Directorate communicates with end-users through a middle man. Specifically, staff in DNDO's planning directorate, not the TAR Directorate, communicate with end-users and then convey these user needs back to the TAR Directorate.

Officials at CBP, a key end-user, told us they would prefer direct communications so they can assure their operational needs and constraints are fully understood during the critical planning stages. Past communication breakdowns between DNDO and CBP highlight the importance of improving this communication channel.

We are continuing our audit work looking at R&D and the TAR Directorate and plan to issue our final report in December.

In summary, DNDO was established to help protect the Nation from the threat and terrible consequences of a nuclear or radiological attack. Improving communication between DNDO and end-users is essential to maximize the chance that its R&D projects will improve the effectiveness of our detection capabilities at the border. Similarly, clearly tracking and documenting how R&D investments address critical gaps in the GNDA will help DNDO demonstrate the benefits of these investments.

Thank you. I would be happy to answer any questions you may have.

[The prepared statement of Mr. Trimble follows:]

PREPARED STATEMENT OF DAVID C. TRIMBLE

JULY 29, 2014

GAO HIGHLIGHTS

Highlights of GAO–14–783T, a testimony before the Subcommittee on Cybersecurity, Infrastructure Protection, and Security Technologies, Committee on Homeland Security, House of Representatives.

Why GAO Did This Study

Preventing terrorists from using nuclear or radiological material to carry out an attack in the United States is a top National priority. Within DHS, DNDO's mission is to: (1) Improve capabilities to deter, detect, respond to, and attribute attacks, in coordination with domestic and international partners, and (2) conduct R&D on radiation and nuclear detection devices. GAO has reported on progress and challenges in DNDO's efforts since 2006 and is currently reviewing DNDO's planning and prioritization of its R&D investments.

This testimony discusses GAO's past work on DNDO's efforts to develop the GNDA and deploy radiation detection equipment and DHS's efforts to coordinate

R&D across the agency, as well as preliminary observations from GAO's on-going review of DNDO's research directorate's efforts to: (1) Manage its R&D investments to align with critical mission needs and (2) coordinate its R&D efforts internally, with other Federal research agencies, and with end-users of the technology it develops.

To conduct its on-going review, GAO analyzed DHS documents and data related to how DNDO plans and prioritizes its R&D program, and interviewed officials on coordinating R&D.

What GAO Recommends

GAO is not making any new recommendations in this statement. As GAO continues to complete its on-going work, it will consider the need for any new recommendations as appropriate. DHS provided technical comments, which were incorporated as appropriate.

COMBATING NUCLEAR SMUGGLING.—PAST WORK AND PRELIMINARY OBSERVATIONS ON RESEARCH AND DEVELOPMENT AT THE DOMESTIC NUCLEAR DETECTION OFFICE

What GAO Found

GAO has reported on the Department of Homeland Security's (DHS) Domestic Nuclear Detection Office (DNDO) since 2006. GAO has identified challenges and made recommendations in the following areas:

- *DNDO's efforts to develop the Global Nuclear Detection Architecture (GNDA).*—In 2008, GAO recommended that DHS develop a strategic plan to guide the development of the GNDA, a framework for 74 independent programs, projects, or activities to detect and interdict nuclear smuggling. In 2010, DHS issued a plan and GAO reviewed this plan and found that it generally addressed GAO's recommendations.
- *DNDO's efforts to replace radiation detection equipment.*—GAO has found challenges in DNDO's efforts to develop and deploy radiation portal monitors, which scan for nuclear or radiological materials at ports of entry. GAO has made several recommendations throughout the history of these efforts, and DNDO has taken actions that have generally been responsive.
- *DHS's efforts to coordinate research and development (R&D) across the agency.*—In 2012 and 2013, GAO made recommendations to help DHS oversee its R&D investments and efforts, and in particular its border and maritime R&D efforts. GAO's recommendations focused on strengthening coordination and defining R&D across the agency. DHS concurred with GAO's recommendations and described actions it plans to take in response.

Preliminary observations from GAO's on-going review are that DNDO has taken steps to manage R&D and assess project outcomes, but that it may not be able to demonstrate how agency investments align with critical mission needs. DNDO officials told GAO that they discuss how research projects may contribute to critical mission needs but that they do not document these discussions. Once research projects are complete, DNDO officials told GAO they evaluate the success of individual research projects, but DNDO does not have a systematic approach to ensure its overall R&D investments address gaps in the GNDA. As a result, DNDO may not be able to demonstrate to key stakeholders—including oversight organizations and potential users of new technologies—that its R&D investments are aligned with critical mission needs.

GAO's on-going work indicates that DNDO officials have taken some steps to coordinate R&D efforts internally, with other Federal agencies, and with end-users, but preliminary analysis shows that not all of DNDO's end-users are satisfied with DNDO's communication. DNDO directorates work closely to identify critical mission needs, and DNDO collaborates with other Federal research agencies to leverage expertise. However, DNDO's end-users varied in their satisfaction with DNDO's efforts to coordinate with them. Officials from two end-user agencies told GAO that coordination was working well; however, officials from the largest end-user agency stated that they were generally dissatisfied with DNDO's coordination because DNDO's research directorate does not provide them information directly and, in some cases, found that project requirements would not meet the agency's operational needs. This is consistent with GAO's 2010 finding that inadequate communication caused DNDO to pursue scanning technology that would not meet the operational requirements of the end-user if it were deployed.

Chairman Meehan, Ranking Member Clarke, and Members of the subcommittee: I am pleased to be here today to discuss our past work on the Department of Homeland Security's (DHS) Domestic Nuclear Detection Office (DNDO) and our preliminary observations on DNDO's management and coordination of its research and development (R&D) investments as you consider the reauthorization of DNDO. Preventing terrorists from using nuclear or radiological material to carry out an attack in the United States is a top National priority. Terrorists could use these materials to make an improvised nuclear device or a radiological dispersal device (also called a "dirty bomb"). The detonation of a nuclear device in an urban setting could cause hundreds of thousands of deaths and devastate buildings and physical infrastructure for miles. While not as damaging, a radiological dispersal device could nonetheless cause hundreds of millions of dollars in socioeconomic costs as a large part of a city would have to be evacuated—and possibly remain inaccessible—until an extensive radiological decontamination effort was completed. A key element of the strategy for protecting the homeland from the consequences of nuclear or radiological terrorism is the Global Nuclear Detection Architecture (GNDA), a multi-layered framework encompassing 74 independent programs, projects, or activities by the Federal Government and its partners to detect and interdict nuclear smuggling in foreign countries, at the U.S. border, and inside the United States.[1]

Within DHS, DNDO is responsible for improving the Nation's capabilities to deter, detect, respond to, and attribute attacks, in coordination with domestic and international partners.[2] To accomplish this, DNDO is organized into directorates that support elements of its mission. Three of these directorates are relevant to my testimony today: (1) The Architecture and Plans Directorate, which analyzes gaps in the GNDA and develops strategies and plans for the GNDA in coordination with its partners; (2) the Product Acquisition and Deployment (Acquisition) Directorate, which is responsible for developing, acquiring, and deploying radiation detection equipment to support the efforts of Federal, State, and local agencies that use radiation detection equipment to carry out their mission; and (3) the Transformational and Applied Research (TAR) Directorate, which conducts R&D of radiation and nuclear detection devices and furthers the development of technologies to support the domestic component of the GNDA. DNDO established the TAR Directorate in 2006 to identify, explore, develop, and demonstrate scientific and technological approaches that meet one or more of the following criteria: Address gaps in the GNDA; improve the performance of domestic radiological and nuclear detection systems and enabling technologies; or increase the operational efficiency of detection technology for domestic end-users: primarily DHS' Customs and Border Protection (CBP), but also Coast Guard, Transportation Security Administration (TSA), and State and local law enforcement. DNDO's TAR Directorate makes R&D investments based on competitive awards to researchers in Government laboratories, academia, and private industry for basic and applied R&D efforts. From fiscal year 2008 through fiscal year 2013, the TAR Directorate obligated approximately $328 million for about 205 projects focused on basic research, technology prototypes, software development, and computer modeling for the detection of radioactive and nuclear materials, among other things. The TAR Directorate's total budget, including R&D, for fiscal year 2014 was $71.1 million.

My testimony today is based on reports we issued from March 2006 to September 2013, as well as preliminary observations from our on-going review for this subcommittee of the TAR Directorate's efforts to plan, prioritize, and assess outcomes of its R&D program. Specifically, my statement today discusses our past work on DNDO's efforts to develop the GNDA and deploy radiation detection equipment and DHS's efforts to coordinate R&D across the agency, as well as preliminary observations from our on-going review of the TAR Directorate's efforts to: (1) Manage its R&D investments to align with critical mission needs, and (2) coordinate its R&D efforts internally, with other Federal research agencies, and with the end-users of the technology it develops.

Detailed information on our scope and methodology for our prior work can be found in the reports cited throughout this statement. To develop our preliminary observations on the TAR Directorate's efforts to manage and coordinate its R&D investments, we reviewed agency documents that identify critical mission needs for R&D and the TAR Directorate's process for planning and prioritizing R&D investments. We also obtained data from the TAR Directorate's project database that contained information on all on-going and completed research projects funded from fiscal year 2008 through 2013, which we used to determine the total number of TAR Directorate research projects and obligations allocated during this period. To assess

---

[1] U.S. Government partners include State, Tribal, and local governments, the private sector, and international partners.

[2] DNDO was established in 2005 by National Security Presidential Directive (NSPD)–43/ Homeland Security Presidential Directive (HSPD)–14 and codified in statute by the Security and Accountability for Every Port Act of 2006 (SAFE Port) Act, Pub. L. No. 109–347 § 501, 120 Stat. 1884, 1932 (codified as amended at 6 U.S.C. § 591).

the reliability of the data, we interviewed the TAR Directorate officials responsible for maintaining the database and determined the data were reliable for providing background information on the TAR Directorate's projects. Our review does not include the TAR Directorate's nuclear forensics portfolio because projects in that portfolio are not selected using the same planning and prioritization process as projects in the TAR Directorate's other research areas. We interviewed the assistant directors of the TAR Directorate, the Architecture and Plans Directorate, and the Acquisition Directorate. We also interviewed the TAR Directorate's research managers on the TAR Directorate's process for identifying critical mission needs, selecting research topics and projects, managing and evaluating research areas, coordinating R&D, and aligning R&D investments with critical mission needs. We also interviewed officials at Federal agencies with a R&D component and potential end-users of technology developed under DNDO's R&D program to understand how DNDO coordinates the planning of R&D. Specifically, we interviewed officials at the Department of Defense's (DOD) Defense Threat Reduction Agency and the Department of Energy's (DOE) National Nuclear Security Administration (NNSA) and end-users at DHS' CBP, the Coast Guard, and TSA to understand their involvement in DNDO's R&D planning, prioritization, and evaluation process. We shared the information on our preliminary findings with officials from DNDO, CBP, Coast Guard, TSA, the Defense Threat Reduction Agency, and NNSA. DNDO and the Defense Threat Reduction Agency officials provided technical comments, which we incorporated, as appropriate. We expect to issue a final report on this work in December 2014.

The work upon which this testimony is based was conducted in accordance with generally accepted Government auditing standards. Those standards require that we plan and perform the audit to obtain sufficient, appropriate evidence to provide a reasonable basis for our findings and conclusions based on our audit objectives. We believe that the evidence obtained provides a reasonable basis for our findings and conclusions based on our audit objectives.

DNDO'S EFFORTS TO DEVELOP THE GNDA AND DEPLOY RADIATION DETECTION EQUIPMENT, AND DHS'S EFFORTS TO COORDINATE R&D

We have reported on progress and challenges in DNDO's efforts to develop the GNDA and deploy radiation detection equipment since 2006 and have recently reported on DHS's efforts to coordinate R&D across the agency.[3]

Regarding DNDO's efforts to develop the GNDA, in July 2008,[4] when DNDO was in the early stages of this work, we found that DNDO, in collaboration with other Federal agencies, had made progress by identifying critical gaps in domestic efforts to prevent and detect radiological and nuclear smuggling but had not clearly articulated a long-term plan for expanding radiological and nuclear detection capabilities to close those gaps. As a result, we recommended that DHS develop a strategic plan to guide the development of the GDNA and, in January 2009, further recommended that DHS develop a strategic plan for the domestic part of the global nuclear detection strategy.[5] DHS has taken actions on these recommendations by issuing an interagency GNDA strategic plan in December 2010 and an implementation plan about 1 year later.[6] In July 2011 and July 2012, when we reviewed these actions, we found that they generally addressed our recommendations.[7] However, in July 2012, we testified that it remained difficult to identify priorities among the components of the domestic part of the GNDA.

Regarding DNDO's efforts to deploy radiation detection equipment, our past work has found challenges in DNDO's efforts to develop and deploy radiation portal mon-

---

[3] See, for example GAO, *Combating Nuclear Smuggling: DHS Has Made Progress Deploying Radiation Detection Equipment at U.S. Ports-of-Entry, but Concerns Remain*, GAO–06–389 (Washington, DC: Mar. 22, 2006); *Nuclear Detection: Preliminary Observations on the Domestic Nuclear Detection Office's Efforts to Develop a Global Nuclear Detection Architecture*, GAO–08–999T (Washington, DC: July 16, 2008); and *Department of Homeland Security: Oversight and Coordination of Research and Development Should Be Strengthened*, GAO–12–837 (Washington, DC: Sept. 12, 2012).

[4] GAO–08–999T.

[5] GAO, *Nuclear Detection: Domestic Nuclear Detection Office Should Improve Planning to Better Address Gaps and Vulnerabilities*, GAO–09–257 (Washington, DC: Jan. 29, 2009).

[6] The GNDA strategic plan was an interagency effort jointly developed by the Departments of Homeland Security, Energy, Defense, Justice, and State; the intelligence community; and the Nuclear Regulatory Commission.

[7] GAO, *Combating Nuclear Smuggling: DHS has Developed a Strategic Plan for its Global Nuclear Detection Architecture, but Gaps Remain*, GAO–11–869T (Washington, DC: July 26, 2011) and *Combating Nuclear Smuggling: DHS has Developed Plans for Its Global Nuclear Detection Architecture, but Challenges Remain in Deploying Equipment*, GAO–12–941T (Washington, DC: July 26, 2012).

itors, which scan for nuclear or radiological materials at ports of entry, at U.S. border crossings, and seaports.[8] As we reported in July 2012, deployed portal monitors are reaching the end of their expected service lives, and DNDO, with input from CBP, will need to make decisions about whether to refurbish or replace them.[9] We have reported, since March 2006, on programs to replace existing portal monitors with more advanced versions and have made several recommendations concerning these efforts, most of which DNDO has implemented.[10] In September 2010, we found that inadequate communication between DNDO and CBP contributed to DNDO pursuing the deployment of a system to use radiography to scan cargo for nuclear materials without fully understanding that it would not fit within existing inspection lanes at ports of entry and would slow down the flow of commerce through these lanes, causing significant delays.[11] At that time, DNDO and CBP officials said they were communicating much more routinely and that, in their view, it would be unlikely that the communication problems we identified would reoccur. DNDO decided to cancel the acquisition of the system and limit any further work on demonstrating the potential capability of the technology to research and development efforts, highlighting the importance of effective coordination even in the R&D phases of a system.

Regarding DHS's efforts to coordinate across its components that conduct R&D, in September 2013 we reviewed the extent to which DHS and its components, including DNDO, coordinated border and maritime R&D efforts within DHS and among other Federal agencies.[12] We found that DNDO has mechanisms for coordinating its R&D efforts that vary depending on the maturity of the technology. Specifically, the TAR Directorate did not always interact directly with DHS' operational components because it worked with less mature technologies. We also found, among other things, that DHS had taken actions to develop Departmental policies to better define and coordinate R&D but that work remained to be done at the agency level to ensure border and maritime R&D efforts are mutually reinforcing and are being directed toward the highest-priority needs. We made recommendations to help ensure that DHS effectively manages and coordinates its border and maritime R&D efforts. DHS concurred with our recommendations and described actions it plans to take in response. In September 2012, we reviewed the management and coordination of R&D at DHS among the Science and Technology Directorate, Coast Guard, DNDO, and other components and found that DHS did not have a Department-wide policy defining R&D or guidance directing components how to report R&D activities and investments.[13] We made recommendations to help ensure that DHS effectively oversees its R&D investments and efforts and reduces fragmentation, overlap, and the risk of unnecessary duplication. As of July 2014, DHS had taken some steps to address two of our recommendations, including establishing a definition of R&D and guidance for coordinating R&D across the agency. However, work remains to be done to address our remaining recommendation to create a mechanism to track existing R&D projects and their associated costs across the Department.

THE TAR DIRECTORATE'S R&D INVESTMENTS MAY NOT ALIGN WITH CRITICAL MISSION NEEDS

Our preliminary observations from our on-going analysis are that DNDO's R&D component, the TAR Directorate, has taken steps to manage R&D and to assess project outcomes, but it may not be able to demonstrate how its R&D investments align with critical mission needs. Each year, the DNDO Architecture and Planning Directorate identifies critical mission needs based on an analysis of gaps in the GNDA and provides this information to the TAR Directorate. According to TAR Directorate officials, research managers within the directorate consider these needs to

---

[8] See, for example, GAO, *Combating Nuclear Smuggling: Additional Actions Needed to Ensure Adequate Testing of Next Generation Radiation Detection Equipment*, GAO–07–1247T (Washington, DC: Sept. 18, 2007); *Combating Nuclear Smuggling: DHS Improved Testing of Advanced Radiation Detection Portal Monitors, but Preliminary Results Show Limits of the New Technology*, GAO–09–655 (Washington, DC: May 29, 2009); and *Combating Nuclear Smuggling: Recent Testing Raises Issues About the Potential Effectiveness of Advanced Radiation Detection Portal Monitors*, GAO–10–252T (Washington, DC: Nov. 17, 2010).

[9] GAO–12–941T.

[10] GAO–06–389.

[11] GAO, *Combating Nuclear Smuggling: Inadequate Communication and Oversight Hampered DHS Efforts to Develop an Advanced Radiography System to Detect Nuclear Materials.* GAO–10–1041T (Washington, DC: Sept. 15, 2010).

[12] GAO, *Department of Homeland Security: Opportunities Exist to Better Evaluate and Coordinate Border and Maritime Research and Development*, GAO–13–732 (Washington, DC: Sept. 25, 2013).

[13] GAO–12–837.

identify the topics for that year's competitive awards for new basic and applied research. After they select which research projects to fund, TAR Directorate officials write contracting documents that guide the goals and milestones of the projects and regularly review the progress of their on-going research projects. According to TAR Directorate officials, they: (1) Consider the potential for the research to contribute to resolving gaps in the GNDA at each step of planning and selecting research projects, and (2) discuss this potential with officials from the other DNDO directorates, the Defense Threat Reduction Agency, and NNSA, but they do not document these discussions. Once research projects are completed, TAR Directorate officials told us they take steps to evaluate the outcomes of individual research projects by, for example, requiring researchers to complete deliverables that describe how the research performed compared with the initial goals for the project that were outlined in the contract.[14]

However, our preliminary observations are that the TAR Directorate has limited information to demonstrate how its R&D investments align with critical mission needs. TAR Directorate officials stated that they understand how projects are intended to make progress on gaps in the GNDA based on the information contained in the contract deliverables of individual projects but acknowledged that it would be difficult for non-scientists who are not fully involved in a project to understand how projects address these gaps based on this information alone. Further, TAR Directorate officials stated that the directorate does not have a systematic approach for evaluating its overall R&D program or a mechanism for: (1) Tracking the longer-term outcomes of individual projects, and (2) measuring how those outcomes may contribute to addressing gaps in the GNDA. TAR Directorate officials told us that the scientific community is small enough that they are usually able to continue to follow their funded research after a project ends. TAR Directorate officials also told us they have made efforts to disseminate the results of individual projects by posting articles on DHS's website and discussing successes at conferences. With limited information on how R&D investments are intended to make progress on gaps in the GNDA, and without a process for assessing and reporting on the results of its R&D program as a whole against those gaps, the TAR Directorate may not be able to demonstrate to key stakeholders—including oversight organizations and potential users of new technologies—that its R&D investments are aligned with critical mission needs. We plan to continue our audit work on this issue and will present our findings in more detail in our final report, with any related suggestions for improvement, which we expect to issue in December 2014.

THE TAR DIRECTORATE HAS TAKEN STEPS TO COORDINATE ITS R&D BUT MAY FACE COMMUNICATION CHALLENGES WITH SOME END-USERS

Our preliminary observations from our on-going analysis are that the TAR Directorate has taken steps to coordinate its R&D efforts internally, with other Federal research agencies, and with end-users of the technologies it develops, but the TAR Directorate may face communication challenges with one of its key end-users. As the TAR Directorate plans and manages its R&D investments, agency officials we interviewed stated that TAR Directorate officials take steps to coordinate within DNDO, across agencies with similar missions, and with potential end-users of resulting technology as follows:

- *Within DNDO.*—Our preliminary observation is that TAR Directorate officials work closely with officials from DNDO's Architecture and Plans Directorate and the Acquisition Directorate to identify critical mission needs based on gaps in the GNDA. For example, according to interviews with officials from all three DNDO directorates, officials from the three directorates participate in and provide feedback to the TAR Directorate during individual project reviews at key milestones and at annual research reviews. In addition, the three directorates coordinate an annual DNDO Industry, Academia, and Lab Engagement Day, formerly known as "industry days" where officials from all three directorates discuss ways to enhance existing radiation detection devices and develop new technologies with members of industry, academia, DOE National laboratories, and others. According to DNDO documents, TAR Directorate officials also share data and results from R&D efforts to inform the acquisition decisions made by the Architecture and Plans Directorate and the Acquisition Directorate. Officials from DNDO's Architecture and Plans Directorate and Acquisition Direc-

---

[14] Our review of the TAR Directorate's R&D projects from fiscal year 2008 through fiscal year 2013 showed that examples of outcomes for completed projects included transferring resulting technology to private industry for commercialization, transitioning knowledge gained to a new TAR Directorate-funded R&D project for further development, or determining that the technology was not feasible.

torate told us that their level of involvement with TAR Directorate officials is effective and provides them with a common understanding of how DNDO's R&D investments are aligned with critical mission needs.

- *Across agencies with similar research missions.*—Our preliminary observation from our on-going review is that the TAR Directorate coordinates regularly with the Defense Threat Reduction Agency and NNSA on both a program and individual project level. According to officials from the TAR Directorate, the Defense Threat Reduction Agency, and from NNSA, this coordination is intended to leverage expertise and decrease the opportunity for duplication of research efforts while each agency invests in areas to meet its mission needs. For example, these officials told us that representatives from these agencies meet regularly to discuss their R&D goals, on-going projects, and topics for soliciting new research.[15] The officials said that the representatives also participate in each other's proposal review processes, as well as project review meetings once funded projects meet key milestones. Officials from the Defense Threat Reduction Agency and from NNSA told us that collaboration with the TAR Directorate works well and keeps them informed about the status and results of relevant research. We plan to continue our audit work on this issue and will present our findings in more detail in our final report, which we expect to issue in December 2014. We reported in June 2014 on collaboration between the Architecture and Plans Directorate and NNSA on an effort to research, develop, and test a new technology for a radiological tracking device and found that although the agencies had been meeting quarterly, this mechanism did not always help them collaborate and draw on each agency's expertise.[16]
- *With potential end-users.*—Our preliminary observation is that the TAR Directorate has an indirect mechanism for coordinating with potential end-users of the technology that the directorate develops during the planning phases of research projects. TAR Directorate officials told us that, rather than communicate directly with end-users, staff in the Architecture and Plans Directorate discuss technology requirements and operational needs with end-users as part of the Architecture and Plans Directorate's work coordinating the GNDA, and these staff relay the information back to the TAR Directorate. Once a project starts, TAR Directorate officials told us they meet directly with end-users by inviting end-users to project review meetings at key milestones, such as technology demonstrations.

In the course of our on-going work, however, we found that end-users' satisfaction with this level of coordination with the TAR Directorate varied. For example, officials from TSA told us that they are generally satisfied with this relationship because they are most interested in acquiring available radiation detection equipment and do not have the technical expertise to engage directly with the TAR Directorate's research efforts. In addition, officials from the Coast Guard told us their indirect relationship with the TAR Directorate works well because it is based on a defined strategy that outlines the Coast Guard's short-term and long-term technology requirements, and the Coast Guard currently has three detailees working at DNDO who are able to communicate the unique needs of the Coast Guard. However, officials from CBP, which is DHS's largest end-user of radiation detection technologies, told us they are generally dissatisfied with the level of interaction with TAR. Specifically, CBP officials stated that they typically do not learn about the TAR Directorate's projects until after the project requirements are written and research contracts are issued and, in some cases, has found that project requirements would not meet CBP's operational needs if the technology were deployed at ports of entry. CBP officials told us they would prefer to work directly with TAR Directorate officials at all stages of the research process to gain a better understanding of the TAR Directorate's research goals and to help ensure that its R&D projects align with CBP's operational needs.

As noted above, in September 2010, we found that poor communication with CBP hampered DNDO's ability to develop an advanced system for detecting nuclear materials.[17] In May 2013, we also found that DNDO's analysis of lessons learned that

---

[15] DNDO has a memorandum of understanding with DOD's Defense Threat Reduction Agency, DOE's NNSA, and the Office of the Director of National Intelligence to coordinate National nuclear detection R&D programs, which, according to officials from all three agencies, guides these efforts.

[16] See GAO, *Nuclear Nonproliferation: Additional Actions Needed to Increase the Security of U.S. Industrial Radiological Sources,* GAO–14–293 (Washington, DC: June 6, 2014). According to TAR Directorate officials, the effort to research, develop, and test a radiological tracking device was not a project within the TAR Directorate.

[17] *GAO–10–1041T.*

it conducted after it canceled an advanced portal monitor program stated that effective outreach, communication, and buy-in from the end-user are critical to successful acquisitions.[18] We plan to continue our audit work on this and other issues and will present our findings in more detail and any related suggestions for improvements in our final report, which we expect to issue in December 2014.

Chairman Meehan, Ranking Member Clarke, and Members of the subcommittee, this completes my prepared statement. I would be pleased to respond to questions that you may have at this time.

Mr. MEEHAN. I want to thank the panelists for their testimony, and I now recognize myself for 5 minutes of questions.

Before I get into some more generalized questions, Dr. Gowadia, could you just take a minute and explain the difference in your mind between what is forensics and what is detection?

Ms. GOWADIA. Certainly, Chairman Meehan.

Detection is, in our parlance, the ability to know that there is nuclear material present. For technical detection, we use this by way of detectors. If you were to use detection writ large, you would say the intelligence community's information would come to bear, law enforcement would come to bear, et cetera. But for nuclear detection, when you say nuclear detection, we literally mean detection by way of instruments to sense the presence of radioactive material.

Forensics, on the other hand, is the ability for us to trace back the material interdicted, or, God forbid, the material detonated, to its origins. So, again, you will hear us talk about the coupling with intelligence and law enforcement to be able to attribute a material to its origin.

Does that help?

Mr. MEEHAN. No, it certainly does, because it could be relevant. You might only have part of a cache of something, and you would then be able to identify where we would be looking for other materials that are of concern. Well, I am grateful for that explanation.

I opened my commentary talking about events in the world. You know, we are watching not just what had been a history of state-sponsored activity in the nuclear era, we have grown up in the world of assured mutual deterrence in which you have major players who have been responsibly balancing each other's presence in some way and we have avoided any kind of a nuclear incident, you know, since the wars.

We are watching other countries develop capacities, including some who currently have them who you worry about whether they become destabilized. But, more recently, just the potential that there are, as I have said, other kinds of both interests on the part of Iran and others to develop nuclear capability as well as nuclear materials, even hospital-grade, but being available to groups that want to do—that aren't necessarily tied directly to nation-states but are terrorist organizations and otherwise who want to do harm or to use those things to leverage their ends.

So we are in a dynamic and complex threat environment, and more than we have ever faced as a Nation. The conditions indicate there is a critical need to bolster homeland security against a threat of terrorism that can be colluded, and we can include this as one of our top priorities.

---

[18] GAO, *Combating Nuclear Smuggling: Lessons Learned from Cancelled Radiation Portal Monitor Program Could Help Future Acquisition*, GAO-13-256 (Washington, DC: May 13, 2013).

So, from your perspective, what actions should DNDO take to bolster the capability to deter and protect against such an attack? In particular, what should DNDO's role be in that regard?

Ms. GOWADIA. Chairman Meehan, you are absolutely right, we are in a dynamic and complex threat environment. Considering the dire consequences of this threat, as you clearly pointed out at the start, we certainly have to be vigilant, remain vigilant, and agile and flexible in our response. So, working with the interagency, we need to continue to plan to be ready for the heightened threat and, again, be ready should the threat be elevated and we get some more credibility and specificity to be agile and responsive.

As the lead Federal agency for coordinating the efforts for the United States Government, our role is predominantly in bringing the community together, setting and shaping the strategy, and making sure that we are operationally ready to respond. Of course, you have entrusted us with precious resources, and we would like to apply them—we will continue to apply them so that we can realize the maximum risk reduction.

Mr. MEEHAN. But how do you mean, sort-of, operationally ready to respond? Because, in reality, we are looking at what is always a threat. The idea of once something has been detected and it is here, if you haven't interdicted it in a certain way prior to its capacity to be operational, then we are already at sort of a too-late point.

So how do we operate in such a way that, you know, the principal objective is to assure that we don't get to the step where we are worried about it being situated and active here in our own homeland?

Ms. GOWADIA. So there are two pieces to this. The first is our strategy, ensuring that we have critical ties to our intelligence community so that we can conduct intelligence-cued searches. Ensuring that our law enforcement partners are well-trained, well-equipped, that is the second piece. Then, of course, there is the technology element, making sure that we have the right technologies so that our law enforcement operators can react when the intelligence cue comes about.

To do this, of course, we must train and exercise constantly. A lot of us hope that in our lifetimes we will never actually have to see this for real. So, to do that, we practice constantly, very remarkably realistic exercises—Federal, State, local, even international partners. We make it so that we are not just exercising the decision-making process but also all the way down to boots on the ground against realistic materials with our red team, realistic materials and interesting configurations, challenging our operators to make that be the case. So that is one piece of it.

I would like to pull the string a little bit on your notion of deterrence for a moment. In the classical sense, nation-states deterrence, we look at it a little differently. Because you would question, how does one deter an enemy who values your death more than their life?

So, for us, there are two pieces of it. Certainly, the forensics element adds a notion of deterrence. If you aid and abet a terrorist, we have the means to trace back to the origin. Then, not so classically, deterrence by denial. Here I will steal something from Mr.

Trimble's colleague, Mr. Maurer, at the GAO, who often says, for detection technology right here at our borders to come into play, we have to have had law enforcement intelligence failures, treaty failures, our partners have had to fail, everything before we get—the security regimes for the material have had to fail, nonproliferation regimes have had to fail, and now we are at our borders with technology.

So it is so important that we build an architecture that is multi-faceted, multi-layered, so that the adversary has to be right every time they encounter any one of these layers, increasing our chances of success and, thus, deterrence by denial.

Mr. MEEHAN. Well, I thank you.

I will turn to the Ranking Member for her questions, but, obviously, we will have the opportunity to go back and forth, and I have some other issues I will follow up with you on.

So, at this point I time, I turn it to the Ranking Member, the gentlelady from New York.

Ms. CLARKE. I thank you, Mr. Chairman.

I thank both of you for your testimony here this afternoon.

I would like to turn to the issue of procurement, because that always tends to be the issue. Last month, DNDO issued a request for proposal for its Human Portable Tripwire Program. As I understand it, these are essentially personal radiation detectors, PRDs, that can also identify the source of radiation. These devices are intended for use by CBP and the Coast Guard. The cost of these devices are going to be $24 million for 26 devices.

I have several questions about this. Let me start with this one: Why are these costs so high? Over $900,000 a piece for something that is worn on an officer's belt. No. 2, do you expect costs to go down for future acquisitions?

No. 3, why are these devices needed? No. 4, in what type of operational environments will these be used? No. 5, why can't traditional PRDs be used in these environments instead?

That is directed to Dr. Gowadia.

Ms. GOWADIA. Thank you, Ranking Member Clarke.

So there is some slight confusion with the announcement. The systems will not cost nearly a million dollars apiece. The ceiling on the contract is $24 million, and our minimum buy is 26. It is not appropriate to divide 24 by 26; that would be incorrect.

We are expecting these devices to cost no more than $10,000. Since it is an active procurement, it would not be appropriate for me to share the Government cost estimate, but we are expecting much lower than $10,000, depending on the capabilities afforded.

Does that give you some pause?

Ms. CLARKE. It does. It does.

Ms. GOWADIA. So, now to your other questions as to the environment and why we need them.

Ms. CLARKE. Uh-huh.

Ms. GOWADIA. These are for our Customs and Border Protection Officers and Coast Guard Officers, as you mentioned. Typically, what happens in DHS operations is you have your pager, your personal radiation detection system, and all it does is detect radiation. Now you need to follow it up with a device that will allow you to distinguish benign from threat, the identification device.

Think of our Border Patrol Officers who are sometimes very far removed from the nearest identification device. So it would be so much more efficient and convenient in their daily operations to have both capabilities built into one. That is what these systems were designed to—detect, identify, and store for archival and retrieval purposes that information on board that system.

So, yes, it would significantly improve our capabilities on the border, improve the efficiency of our operations, and, I think, alleviate some of the operational burden for our staff.

Ms. CLARKE. Very well. Are you confident that the technologies to, sort-of, have that 3-in-1 capability already exist?

Ms. GOWADIA. So we have looked at through a lot of our testing certain spectroscopic pagers, particularly in the testing we did with our European Commission partners overseas in the ITRAP+10 test series. We will use those data to make our assessments.

Again, since this is an active and open——

Ms. CLARKE. Right.

Ms. GOWADIA [continuing]. Procurement, I think my procurement officer would get really upset with me if I were to say very much more.

Ms. CLARKE. Very well, Dr. Gowadia.

To radiation portal monitors—and this is for both Dr. Gowadia and Mr. Trimble. Like many on this committee, we cannot and should not forget some of the wasteful acquisitions and deployments of complex security hardware that did not meet the needs of the threat or meet requirements of the program it was intended for. The ASP program is one of those.

Would you give us an overview today of the status of the ASP program and later give us written details as to the cost and the planning documents that will describe the details of the current posture of the ASP within your planning strategies?

Ms. GOWADIA. As you are aware, Ms. Clarke, the program was started in 2004 and cancelled in 2011.

To make the best use of the technologies that we had procured, the low-rate initial production units, 36 of those systems are—we gave them to universities and National laboratories to continue with the science, and some fraction of those were also shared with the Department of Energy's Second Line of Defense Program. They continue to be operated in the field for overseas scanning operations.

Five of those portal monitors were given to our States—Georgia, Tennessee, Mississippi, Missouri, and New Mexico. Two more are on their way to California.

For the mobile detectors, the ones that were built onto trucks, essentially SUVs, we have some in New York, some in Virginia, and some in Alabama and Florida. So seven of nine mobile detection systems are also in use today.

These systems have served as a means for us to gather important technical data—operational data and maintenance data. They will certainly factor into all our technology programs moving forward, our acquisition programs moving forward. In fact, they will inform our analysis of alternatives for whatever we will do next with our radiation portal monitors.

But, most importantly, we have learned our lessons well on the cancellation, the acquisition process. We have turned up the discipline at DNDO so that we have a very rigorous solution development process, which is aligned very nicely with the Department's Acquisition 102–01. We are beginning to share our integrated governance and program management approach across the Department, in concert with the Secretary's unity-of-effort priority, as well as the establishment of the Joint Requirements Council at the Department. So we hope that the lessons we have learned will inform not just us, as they have, but across the DHS acquisition community.

Mr. TRIMBLE. I don't have too much to add to that. A lot of our work is a couple years old, at this point. I think what I would highlight is, just sort of from the lessons learned from that experience, the importance of communication between end-users and the developers of the system, that that is absolutely critical at all phases.

Not particular to DNDO, I would note that we did a wrap-up report, I believe in 2013, looking at the lessons learned from the ASP program. One of our recommendations from that was to DHS to—they have a policy for doing lessons learned, but they didn't have a process to make sure their components were actually following it. So, as Dr. Gowadia mentions that they are trying to implement these lessons, we had a recommendation to make sure that that kind of thing was happening across DHS, because there was not a real disciplined process to make sure that was happening.

Ms. CLARKE. Thank you, Mr. Chairman. Yield back.

Mr. MEEHAN. I thank the gentlelady.

Dr. Gowadia, in the commentary both from my colleague as well as some of the opening statements and certainly some of the other written testimony, DNDO has been described before as "soup-to-nuts," in a larger way, maybe, than some other agencies. So you start with basic research, all the way through to participating in the deployment and even the operations with your stakeholder.

So explain to me your approach to research and development and then how that is tied to your critical needs. But just as significantly, because I think some of the testimony we had before, how about the gaps? How is this focused on filling those gaps so that we ultimately have this turning into, you know, operational systems and procedures that work and that are cost-effective?

Ms. GOWADIA. Yes, certainly, Chairman Meehan.

In thinking through the soup-to-nuts approach, as a result of developing the strategy, the Global Nuclear Detection Architecture strategy, and all the work that we have done so far over our last 9 years, the authorities you have afforded us by way of the SAFE Port Act, I think, are a very effective means for us to combat nuclear terrorism. You have given us a singular focus, making it so that we stay on target every day for a threat that has a very low probability, very high consequences.

The holistic, integrated approach, I think, is valuable because we are interested in moving capability to the field. Capability is so much more than just technology. It is the training. It is the exercises. It is, as you mentioned very appropriately, ensuring that we analyze the risk, establish the gaps, and allocate our resources in accordance with them. We do this through our R&D program, through our test and evaluation that supports the R&D, and certainly through our operations support program.

So I want to dispel the notion that we are an operational office. We are not. But we are very keenly supportive of our operational partners. To Ms. Clarke's point, we bring in our operational partners very early. We are an interagency office. We were established that way for a purpose. We do not just have scientists and engineers; we have intelligence officers, we have retired intelligence officers, retired law enforcement officers, policy analysts, acquisition professionals——

Mr. MEEHAN. But where do you draw the distinction between your group and the operational entities? Who are some of those? Are those the port entities themselves, among others?

Ms. GOWADIA. Yes. Yes, sir. So we do the risk analysis and, with them, develop the right technologies, with them, test the right technologies.

Mr. MEEHAN. Which is the improvement you are looking on incorporating——

Ms. GOWADIA. Exactly.

Mr. MEEHAN [continuing]. In, so we avoid the mistakes that led to the first overruns that the Ranking Member has discussed.

Ms. GOWADIA. Exactly, Mr. Meehan. In doing so, we are able to develop and buy the right systems for them that are suited to their CONOPS. Now, who are they? Customs and Border Protection, Coast Guard, TSA, our State and local law enforcement operators, our international partners. We do the R&D for across the enterprise even though we don't buy for across the enterprise.

Mr. MEEHAN. Right.

Broadening on the enterprise, we have discussed the concept of nuclear, and that is a large part of the focus, but you work in combination on which we are dealing with a number of weapons of mass destruction that we are concerned about, not just analysis but preparedness, response, again, the soup-to-nuts to these kinds of major challenges. The Integrated Terrorism Risk Assessment looks at things like chemical, biological, radiological, as well as nuclear threats.

So what are your contributions to the risk assessment piece, in the first part? How is your collaboration working, particularly with the areas of chem and bio that are part of, you know, what is going on with the Department of Homeland Security?

Ms. GOWADIA. Our contributions to the Presidentially-mandated Integrated Terrorism Risk Assessment is the rad/nuke piece. We collaborate with our partners at S&T, S&T Directorate, who do the chem and bio pieces. These come together to form that integration.

Chairman Meehan, I would posit that this is an excellent example of how we can bring unity of effort to bear within the Department—again, something the Secretary has stressed upon—S&T and DNDO's analytical capabilities brought to bear to inform and influence and assist our operational partners as they allocate their resources, not just at DHS but also in the interagency.

Mr. MEEHAN. Well, how have you been able to see that mature and grow?

So often, what we see has been competition or, you know, misdirection even from groups within agencies that sit side-by-side that see themselves having a little bit of a different mission or a simultaneous mission, in essence, but a different subset of it, and, you know, sometimes we break into rivalries.

How has it been that it has been able to work effectively in this fashion, where you have been able to create a common objective?

Ms. GOWADIA. I think it has been mostly because we have very clear lanes. We are responsible for the rad/nuke piece. We have developed a construct that you have seen—and, Ms. Clarke, I would love for you to see at your convenience—a construct that looks at the risk by virtue of a layered transportation model.

We have figured out how to work with our National laboratories to get the right weapons information, the right radiological threat information. We couple that with an adversary model that uses game theory as well as probabilistic risk assessments. Using that, we are able to lay down 394 nodes in the architecture and score each one, allowing us to have a framework for gaps.

Now, that construct works for the rad/nuke effort. For the chem effort and the bio effort, you need different constructs.

At the working level, repeat constantly to make sure that our inputs can then be coordinated. Different constructs can still render results in a similar way to be integrated moving forward.

Mr. MEEHAN. Well, you identified how you addressed the gaps just in the nuclear side alone——

Ms. GOWADIA. Yes, sir.

Mr. MEEHAN [continuing]. But the same concept, then, is worked to assure that we are doing the same thing with the other kinds of WMD?

Ms. GOWADIA. Yes. So for the chemical piece—and I don't want to speak too far out of my lane here—for the chem piece, they look at things differently because they have a different set of challenges by way of their toxins. In the biological realm, their risks are driven differently.

So we each arrive at common factors that can be rolled up into the integrated risk assessment, mostly based on frequency of probable attack, dollar values of consequences, et cetera. These things are integrated to allow, for instance, HHS to plan countermeasures, medical countermeasures.

Mr. MEEHAN. Right. Right. Well, I thank you.

My time has expired for this particular round, so I am going to turn it back to my colleague.

Ms. CLARKE. Thank you, Mr. Chairman.

I want to pick up on one of the themes you raised about duplicating efforts. The National Nuclear Security Agency, NNSA, has a nuclear forensic mission to collect detailed information on nuclear material from across the world. DNDO also has a nuclear forensics mission.

What is DNDO's forensics mission, and how is it different from NNSA's? In what areas within the forensic mission does DNDO take a leadership role, and what areas does NNSA take a leadership role? Are there areas where the missions of NNSA and DNDO overlap?

I want to hear from both you, Dr. Gowadia and Mr. Trimble.

Mr. TRIMBLE. So, in the area of forensics, this is not an issue, especially in regards to, sort-of, roles and responsibilities across the agencies, that we have looked at. We have had internal discussions that this might be an area for us to discuss with potential Hill clients; it is worthy of an inquiry.

But we have done, and I have in my portfolio, NNSA, and we have done some Classified work regarding, sort-of, accountability of some of the nuclear materials overseas as well as some of the forensics. But we haven't done, sort-of, a cross-agency.

The agency you didn't mention was also DOD plays in this sandbox, as well.

Ms. CLARKE. Uh-huh.

Ms. GOWADIA. Well, for us, in the nuclear forensics realm, we have much the same coordination responsibilities as we have discussed on the detection side.

The forensics mission can be divided up into pre-detonation or post-detonation forensics. In the pre-detonation world, we could either capture material or a full device. DNDO is uniquely responsible for the pre-detonation materials element, so the technical capabilities we need to attribute the materials to their source. DOE is responsible for the pre-detonation weapon itself. The FBI and DOD, depending on whether it is CONUS or OCONUS, are responsible for the post-det side. So that is how we have nicely broken up the space, so to speak.

We could not, again, do this without our intelligence community underpinning and the strong support of our National laboratories system. So we work together to make sure that we have a common strategic plan. We do. We have just set up a requirements center, which we co-chair with the FBI, to make sure that we have our strategic priorities lined up right.

The thing that you have given us uniquely, by virtue of law, is to establish a nuclear forensics expertise development pipeline program. Many years ago, this was, as I mentioned in my opening statement, an in extremis capability. We did not have enough graduate students in our universities across the country studying the appropriate sciences—radiochemistry, for example.

We have turned that around. We have established a really good pipeline. Nineteen of these students that have come all the way through are now already in the laboratories, and we will have 35 by 2018. So we have gone from 4 in radiochemistry a few years ago to suddenly looking at 35 down the line.

Ms. CLARKE. Well, that is very impressive, Dr. Gowadia.

Let me just close with this question, and it is about red-teaming covert rad/nuke testing. DNDO has a red-teaming directorate that independently assesses the performance of planned and deployed capabilities, including technologies and procedures.

A recent GAO report on CBP covert testing of its rad/nuke detection capabilities found that DNDO only works one to three times a year with CBP on conducting these types of tests.

Why isn't the DNDO red-teaming directorate more involved with the CBP covert testing program? Is this a risk-based decision? Is it because of resource constraints?

Ms. GOWADIA. Ma'am, when it comes to our red-teaming efforts, we support much more than our Customs and Border Protection partners. We certainly value their partnership, but we also have to extend that capability to our State and local partners, our interagency partners—DOD, FBI, et cetera, DOE. We also work with Coast Guard and TSA in some of those efforts.

So, yes, actually, it just comes down to these things take a very long time to develop and build and execute. That is not where it ends. We have to come back, learn our lessons, turn it around into documented steps for improvement. So that entire process takes a good bit of time. We are able to sustain about, I want to say around 20 operations a year, overt and covert.

Ms. CLARKE. Did you want to add anything to that?

Mr. TRIMBLE. I am a little limited in what I can say about that recent report. It was issued Friday, but it is restricted. So I would be happy to answer questions on it, but it was largely focused on CBP, and there were issues about prioritization raised in that. But I would be happy to, in another forum, discuss that in more detail.

Ms. CLARKE. Very well.

Thank you, Mr. Chairman. I yield back.

Mr. MEEHAN. I thank the gentlelady.

Mr. Trimble, you just talked about CBP, which brings to mind a report the GAO had done in 2012 looking at opportunities, you know, across the board to reduce duplication, achieve savings, and enhance revenue. But it also identified that there was no single recognized agency responsible for leading and directing Federal efforts to combat nuclear smuggling.

Do you feel that there is any kind of fragmentation in these efforts to combat those nuclear threats? If so, are there possible solutions or better consolidation, or are the responsibilities, do you think, better articulated now since the report in 2012?

Mr. TRIMBLE. Yeah, what I would—and I would have to take that for a more full answer for the record. I would have to look at the specifics on the 2012 report you are referring to.

The broader issue of overlapping duplication I know was raised in a recent report. We looked at DHS for their R&D program in science and technology, where we raised concerns about DHS not having a common definition of what research and development meant and then having a common reporting guidance so that research and development across DHS could be managed to avert potential duplication across all the R&D activities within DHS.

Because within DHS you have several components that have statutory authority to do R&D. It sort-of has the deconfliction/coordination role, and it was having challenges doing that because there wasn't a common shared understanding of it and there wasn't common procedures on how the reporting could go.

Mr. MEEHAN. Well, in such a narrowly-focused—and I don't mean the importance of this is narrowly-focused, but the issue itself is somewhat focused, narrowly-focused—how do you assure that we are prioritizing R&D and making sure that there is collaboration so that there isn't duplication or something being done over here that is of no benefit to what you consider to be a priority?

Mr. TRIMBLE. Yeah, well, that is a great question, and that ties very closely to the observations from our current work.

As my statement said, what we are finding is that DNDO has mechanisms to help coordinate and manage their R&D. Where we are—you know, again, preliminary observations, but where we are seeing a potential for improvement is tracking the specific projects back to the gaps. So you have gaps, you create research priorities, then you create—they have grand challenges, and then you create portfolios of research, and then you actually have the project.

So they are very good at managing through that to the projects and then assessing how you did at the projects at the end of the year. But there is the risk—and I don't want to make it oversimplified, but it is the forest-for-the-trees risk, right? You get to this point, but are you forgetting where you started?

It is just making that—so what our initial observations are, making that linkage back from the specific project you funded to your big need could be better documented. We think, overall, there needs to be a process for the whole portfolio to evaluate how your R&D effort is going.

That is sort-of where we are going with our on-going work. Again, it is preliminary, but the folks are coordinating, there is documentation, they say they understand the linkages, they say it is in the contract documentation and the project documentation. But unless you are a scientist, it is really difficult to come in and say, yeah, we are doing great or we are off-track.

Mr. MEEHAN. But that is something you are, more or less, currently looking at?

Mr. TRIMBLE. That reflects our, sort-of, current thinking on the job today.

Mr. MEEHAN. Well, we look forward to your thinking as you draw some of your conclusions.

Let me ask you another question, too, about the reality that—well, we talk about nation-states and the concern that there could be materials that would find their way, you know, old Russian weapons or other things that get into the hand of terrorist organizations like Hamas or otherwise. But there are a lot of other high-risk industrial sources of radiological materials, including mobile and stationary sources. We have an inside threat because of their presence here.

So how does DNDO work with the other groups in charge of this, you know, the Nuclear Regulatory Commission, the NNSA, and others, to secure these materials and prevent theft? Do you think that is being adequately done?

Mr. TRIMBLE. Yeah, well, interestingly, Dr. Gowadia and I testified about a month ago on this very subject, on securing industrial sources in the United States. GAO has done a couple of reports. Previously, we did a report looking at securing medical sources of radiological materials.

I will let Dr. Gowadia talk to you on her role in that process, but what I would highlight from our recent work on this is that it is really an NRC licensing issue, because NRC is setting the rules by which users of the radiological materials in the United States must secure these materials. What our report had found was that the NRC guidance and requirements could be improved with more specificity.

So, for example, the regs in the NRC vein would say, you must use a lock to secure this radiological material in your truck. Well, a lock can be like a simple high school gym locker lock or it can be a secure, nice security lock. When we went out in the field, as you might expect, everyone is doing something different.

Mr. MEEHAN. Uh-huh.

Mr. TRIMBLE. Similarly, they had regulations concerning co-location, like, what would trigger—say you have sources of material. If you put them in individual cubbies, locks, you didn't hit the regulatory threshold to have security measures. So, for well logging companies, they could have a very large amount of radiological material but not have to implement security measures. So we had very pointed recommendations regarding that.

The other area, on insider threat, very notable in that report. It was that we found an instance where someone with two convictions for making terroristic threats had been given unescorted access to radiological materials. The NRC—to acknowledge that that was okay by their regulations.

Mr. MEEHAN. Well, I mean, for materials like this, no matter where they are, if they are in an industrial setting like a hospital or in, you know, a Government facility, isn't there some level of requirement before you have access to those kinds of things, that you pass some sort of background——

Mr. TRIMBLE. Well, that—right. That is the NRC—NRC sets those requirements, and NRC licenses the material. But the licensing requirements are very general. Then the background check provisions are essentially to say fingerprint, do a background check, but there are no "thou shall nots" in the requirements. So even if you do a background check and you find someone has an extensive criminal record, it is still okay, it is still the company's decision whether to grant that person access.

The connection I would make—I mean, it is a little—the connection I would—and I made it at the last hearing—is the importance of that is, as Dr. Gowadia tightens the noose and makes it more difficult to come into this country with these materials, it makes it much even more appealing to go domestic, shop local for your dirty-bomb material, than try to bring it in from overseas.

So it is the other side of the equation, right? Your instinct is right on this, is, as you make it harder to make this stuff come in for the United States, you can't neglect how easy it is to get it domestically.

Mr. MEEHAN. Dr. Gowadia, what do you think about that and the concept—I mean, I get it, I don't want to micromanage to that level. But, you know, we prevent people who have spent their whole college career and they can't get a teaching degree because they had a marijuana thing in their background. Other policy, other place, some other time. But that is prevention. It seems to me that if you have a criminal record and the record relates to some kind of, you know, threats or otherwise, to be able to have any access to materials is mind-boggling to me.

But you can react to other points of Mr. Trimble's commentary, as well as that particular issue, if you would.

Ms. GOWADIA. Certainly, Chairman Meehan, the more secure these materials are, the easier it becomes on us. That layered, multifaceted architecture that begins with the material security is reinforced. So anything any of us can do to continue to, as Mr. Trimble mentioned, to tighten that noose, no matter where you are in the chain, would certainly have beneficial cascading effects to prevent a successful nuclear or radiological attack.

Securing the materials themselves is not within DNDO's purview. We are recipients of the information once it has left regulatory control, and so we have a very close ties with our partners at NRC. In fact, NRC sends us a detailee, and DOE, on occasion, has sent us detailees, so that we can maintain some of that ongoing dialogue and awareness of an on-going event.

It is my understanding that both the NRC and DOE have accepted Mr. Trimble's recommendations.

Mr. TRIMBLE. I would say a qualified accept.

Ms. GOWADIA. Qualified.

But we will certainly partner with them and watch the implementation and encourage best practices to be shared. It can only improve the security.

Mr. MEEHAN. Right. I thank you.

Well, let me turn to the gentlelady for a final question.

Ms. CLARKE. Very well, Mr. Chairman.

Just an ask of you, Dr. Gowadia, if you have a list of authorities or program changes that you think are needed that the subcommittee can be of assistance with, we would ask that you submit that to us in writing, especially considering the likelihood that in the upcoming years we will be seeing some declining budgets. We want to make sure that, to the extent that we can make the case for maintenance of effort, at least, that we have all of the information that helps us to make the case.

Ms. GOWADIA. Certainly. Certainly, Ms. Clarke. We definitely will do that. We will send you our request in writing.

We have reviewed our authorities. We don't see the need to expand them. We do feel that the set, as they are, are extremely valuable. They are manifest in every day that we do our work.

The only request we really have is to change one of our reporting requests from an annual to a biennial status. It would allows us to save just at DNDO $800,000 every 2 years if we were to go into that cadence. It would actually be more meaningful, because the progress—it is hard to see it year on year, but giving us a longer integration time, I think, would be more valuable to you, as well. So that one our one request.

There are other things on the margins which we will certainly share with all of you and your staff. Again, thank you very much for affording us the opportunity to have this reauthorization, and we look forward to working with you to move forward on it.

Ms. CLARKE. Very well.

I yield back, Mr. Chairman.

Mr. MEEHAN. I thank the gentlelady.

Let me just ask one, sort-of, closing question or comment, Dr. Gowadia, because you have been at this for a short period of time, but you project, as well.

I think if we look at this, just in the 4 years that I have been here, we have seen a change in the global environment. We have seen more concern about terrorist organizations and others who seem to be getting more active and potentially have access to things. We have seen Iran in a state in which not only are we worried about the proliferation of their capacity, and there are political questions about how well-contained that will be, but it is—I hope it is not predictable, but it is foreseeable that if there is any on-going Iranian capacity to continue to expand, that you might begin to see proliferation of other countries looking, either because they want to participate or they want to protect themselves by at least having an equal status. We could see, down the road, not just a few but numbers of countries, in fact even potentially scores of countries, with access to nuclear capacity, maybe even nuclear weapons.

So, anticipating the combination of the threat of terrorism and the loose—the struggle we have to prevent things being controlled, I should say, not loose, but be in control of that which exists, and the concern about proliferation and new states, where do you see your mission evolving in, you know, 5 and 10 years compared to where you began with some of this? What other kinds of challenges do you think you might face in the future?

Ms. GOWADIA. Chairman Meehan, our vision will remain the same: A Nation secure from the threat of nuclear terrorism. But we will continue with our interagency partners, our State and local partners, our international partners to continue to build this multilayered, multifaceted architecture, again, to make it so that the undertaking of such an act would just be prohibitively difficult.

Now, it goes all the way back to the security of materials, the spreading of best practices. We will continue to work with our international partners at the IAEA, the National Law Enforcement Agency, even partner nations, so that they begin to develop, based on our best practices and guidelines, what we have learnt, readily to share their other own architectures. So as you have National architectures built up—and by that, I don't just mean detection systems, I mean regulatory infrastructure, just as we have with the NRC—good practices for securing and maintaining their materials, accountability, et cetera, developing interior law enforcement capabilities within the nations, not just border capabilities, this begins to set up a harder and harder challenge, so even if we do see the proliferation, we continue on the blue side to improve capabilities.

Now, speaking of proliferation, you know that President Obama has laid strong priority in reducing the amount of special nuclear material that is available in the world today. We have made tremendous progress based on the security summits that he started. I don't have all the facts with me just yet off the top of my head, but I do believe the nation-states that had special nuclear materials significantly reduced in the last 6 years. I hope that trend continues. Best practices that DOE shares and DOD shares with their partner nations, again, for the security of the military programs, is so important.

Again, multiple layers, multi-faceted layers. If you choose to do this, we can look at the money transfers, we can look at the SIGINT, et cetera, et cetera. Anything that would give us an advantage and an edge and make it so they have to be right every time, giving us better opportunity, is exactly where we are headed.

Can't do this without our partners. Our greatest focus will be our partners. We have found a way to include them in all our activities, all our planning from Day 1, whether it is the risk assessment, the capabilities-based assessments. They write the mission needs statements with us. That is a significant lesson learned from our past missteps.

So those partnerships—law enforcement, operational community, intelligence community, technical community—we will base our efforts moving forward, particularly in light of the diminishing budget. We don't have the luxury of having any overlap. We will have to strategically partner to advance the cause, even partnering with our international partners. We have the British collaborating with us in R&D with S&T. So anywhere where we can find a way to leverage, we must and will do so.

Mr. MEEHAN. Well, I applaud you for that leveraging with the friendly partners in the international community. It seems to make sense for all of us to be doing so in that capacity.

So I want to thank you again for your leadership.

I want to thank you, Mr. Trimble, for your oversight.

Collectively, these are continuing explorations of very, very vitally important issues to not only our homeland security but actually global security. So I thank you for your work and your valuable testimony.

It is possible that some of our Members who will read this transcript will be interested in having additional questions. So if they do, you know, we ask that you respond in writing.

But I thank you again for your testimony.

Without objection, the subcommittee stands adjourned.

[Whereupon, at 3:15 p.m., the subcommittee was adjourned.]

APPENDIX

Question 1. What is DNDO's relationship with the DOE labs, and how is DNDO leveraging their capabilities and expertise? Are there lessons learned in contracting with the labs that would be beneficial to other DHS organizations?

Answer. The Domestic Nuclear Detection Office (DNDO) has a good working relationship with the Department of Energy (DOE) National Laboratories and they have made significant contributions to all aspects of the DNDO mission. According to the Homeland Security Act, DNDO (as part of DHS) has access to the laboratories equal to that of DOE; DHS-funded activity is not considered to be "work for others" that the labs can refuse if they don't think it to be within their mission. In fiscal year 2013, DNDO obligated over $72 million at the DOE National Laboratories and will likely obligate over $82 million in fiscal year 2014.

National Laboratory subject-matter experts' knowledge of nuclear weapons and associated capabilities has been a great asset to DNDO. Their staff provides key data and analysis into system threat reviews, including on-going analyses that are being used to determine the feasibility of reconfiguring radiation portal monitor settings to reduce the number of nuisance alarms while maintaining threat detection sensitivity. We also rely on their unique knowledge and expertise to design, manufacture, store, and transport the special nuclear materials and weapon mock-ups (test sources) that we use in our test campaigns and red teaming.

In fact, testing and evaluation of nuclear detection systems is a key area where DNDO leverages DOE National Laboratory facilities and expertise. Scientists from the National Laboratories help us to design tests that are rigorous but efficient, with many of these test campaigns conducted at DOE facilities. For example, our Radiological and Nuclear Countermeasures Test and Evaluation Complex is located at the Nevada National Security Site, a DOE facility. Its location, adjacent to DOE's Device Assembly Facility, allows us to utilize the unique sources stored at this facility. Nevada National Security Site personnel maintain and secure our test facility, and also provide staff to execute our tests.

Many of the National Laboratories support cutting-edge research to develop new capabilities for nuclear threat detection. This research spans such broad areas as advanced materials for gamma-radiation detection, new approaches to neutron detection and other novel techniques for radiation detection, gamma-ray imaging, advanced techniques for the active detection of shielded nuclear materials, and improved capabilities for modeling and simulation to understand detector performance.

To fulfill its technical nuclear forensics mission, DNDO also relies on the National Laboratories. Nearly all research and development to improve technical nuclear forensics is conducted at DOE National Laboratories, and we work with them on our National Technical Nuclear Forensics Expertise Development Program to increase the number of scientists capable of conducting the National technical nuclear forensics.

Finally, DNDO was established in the Department of Homeland Security as an interagency organization that may receive detailed personnel from the Secretary of Defense, the Secretary of Energy, the Secretary of State, the Attorney General, the Nuclear Regulatory Commission, and the directors of other Federal agencies, including elements of the intelligence community. Traditionally DNDO has also benefited from the inclusion of National Laboratory employees through Intergovernmental Personnel Agreements (IPAs). This year, DNDO has had three IPAs working as a part of our staff—one from Oak Ridge National Laboratory, one from Lawrence Livermore National Laboratory, and one from Los Alamos National Laboratory.

When contracting with the DOE labs, DNDO has found it beneficial to provide the DOE site office with advanced notification of pending interagency agreements. This allows us to identify and make any necessary changes to the Statement of Work prior to approval by a DHS contracting officer and submission to DOE. Advanced notification jump-starts the DHS and DOE review and approval processes and shortens the time to codify the interagency agreement.

Question 2a. Research projects are inherently risky—with great uncertainty about the end results of the research. Because of this risk, sometimes research projects fail to produce intended results. In some respects, this is part of the cost of doing research.

Does DNDO have any kind of a benchmark for what percentage of research projects should end in positive results—meaning that the research leads to the development of a new or improved capability?

Question 2b. How does the Congress know if it is getting an appropriate yield for its investment in DNDO R&D activities?

Answer. In order to tackle our technical grand challenges while providing near-term results, DNDO takes a balanced approach to technical risk. To that end, DNDO's R&D budget supports approximately 20% basic research, 40% applied research, and 40% technology development. This approach also supports the establishment of a healthy technology development pipeline. On a regular basis, all projects report out their R&D results, either positive or negative, so that the body of knowledge is continuously increasing.

In addition, annually DNDO reports two DHS management performance measures that demonstrate a robust technology pipeline and a robust human capital, or workforce, pipeline.

- For the technology pipeline, in 2013 DNDO obtained 42 comprehensive evaluations or demonstrations of new and improved technologies to protect against nuclear terrorism, surpassing its goal of 23.
- For the human capital pipeline, in 2013 DNDO granted 71 student fellowships and faculty awards in nuclear forensics and radiation detection-related specialties, surpassing its goal of 63.

DNDO works closely with DHS Program Analysis and Evaluation and the Office of Management and Budget to develop performance measures and set targets. The targets reflect projected outcomes based on Department priorities and budgetary considerations.

Over the period of multiple years, the success of an R&D program can be demonstrated by technology that transitioned from an idea, to a laboratory prototype, to a new operational capability. DNDO has implemented rigorous processes to track the progress of individual research efforts by using technology readiness levels, feasibility evaluations, proof-of concept demonstrations, and technology demonstration and characterizations. DNDO also employs a phase-based approach to research management, where progress is assessed for a given project after every phase in the project's life cycle to determine whether the research should be carried forward or discontinued, and all portfolios are periodically reviewed by the DNDO leadership team. These processes allow for economy and efficiency in research execution, mitigate technical risk, and permit focusing research to productive end-states. We are presently working to comprehensively summarize the transition success of our portfolio, and early indications are that it is on par or above the success of other Federally-sponsored research programs.

DNDO is beginning to see the results of technology transfers resulting in the fielding of detection capabilities. As a result of DNDO's efforts, there are new gamma-ray detection materials, new neutron detectors that are not dependent on Helium–3 (a rare material in very short supply that is being reserved for applications in which it cannot be replaced), improved algorithms, and modeling tools that are now either commercial products or are broadly available to support the research and development community as a whole. Technologies supporting long-range radiation detection and wide-area search operations have also been matured to the point where programs of record and commercial spin-offs are feasible.

Finally, new technologies for the detection of shielded special nuclear material in cargo continue to mature, and several have or are achieving significant maturity to support operational demonstrations. Together, these successes contribute to improved capabilities, and create core technologies that will support a range of future capabilities.

Question 3. The National Technical Nuclear Forensics Center was established within DNDO in October 2006. As you know, the mission is to serve as program integrator and steward for the U.S. Government to ensure a ready, robust, and enduring nuclear forensics capability. Can you update us on this program and has it been successful? How do you measure that success?

Answer. DNDO has had considerable success with our nuclear forensics mission. Since 2006, when DNDO was given this mission, the U.S. Government has made substantial progress in developing requirements, addressing technology gaps, improving the rigor of exercises, and increasing the expertise pipeline from academia to the National Laboratories. DNDO has worked to coordinate the efforts of the U.S. Government for planning, operations, and technology development in nuclear forensics and attribution.

Today the interagency constantly plans together, through Executive Council and Steering Committee meetings at DNDO and many other planning venues. We develop joint plans, such as the 2010 National Strategic Five-Year Plan for Improving the Nuclear Forensics and Attribution Capabilities of the United States.

We established a Nuclear Forensics Requirements Center, which DNDO co-chairs with the Federal Bureau of Investigation Laboratory. For the first time, we've identified, developed, and documented technical and operational requirements across the nuclear forensics spectrum.

Technical capabilities are steadily advancing. For example, DNDO has developed the first-ever lab-scale uranium processing capability to determine nuclear material characteristics that are uniquely associated with specific variations of uranium manufacturing processes. This capability allows us to better link the material to its origin and possible pathways.

Forensics exercises have become remarkably realistic and rigorous, with intensive multi-agency planning among the Federal Bureau of Investigation, the Department of Energy, the Department of Defense, and DNDO. Many of the exercises now include State and local law enforcement. State and local law enforcement have provided facilities for exercises, as well as air transport and safety escorts for the nuclear forensics teams to collect simulated debris samples for nuclear forensic analysis.

Another notable success is our Expertise Development program, which was launched in 2008. To date, we have provided support to over 300 undergraduate and graduate students, as well as faculty members at 23 universities. Nineteen new nuclear forensics Ph.D. scientists have come through our "pipeline program" and been hired, primarily by the DOE National Laboratories, since the program's inception. This brings us more than halfway to our goal of adding 35 new Ph.D. scientists into the nuclear forensics field by 2018.

We have a variety of methods for measuring our progress in executing the technical nuclear forensics mission.

First, we assess our progress in an Annual Report to Congress against the objectives laid out in the National Strategic Five-Year Plan. Further, the annual National Technical Nuclear Forensics Implementation Plan describes how the community will accomplish the objectives outlined in the Strategic Plan.

Second, with respect to technical capability development, DNDO focuses on providing our operational partners with the ability to accurately and precisely measure and characterize nuclear and other radioactive materials in a defensible manner that will stand up to outside and legal scrutiny. Guiding this effort is a set of measurement requirements authored by the interagency Bulk Special Nuclear Material Analysis Program. DNDO develops analytical methods to meet these requirements, and measures success in the transition of approved methods to the DOE's operational nuclear forensics laboratories.

Third, in the exercise arena, we have a formal process for evaluating technical competencies and areas for improvement during exercises. These areas for improvement are discussed among the partner agencies and documented in Corrective Action Plans, which are implemented, tracked, and verified in subsequent exercises.

Fourth, for expertise development, we closely track the numbers of students, colleges, and junior faculty members receiving awards, and we monitor their progress through our pipeline in conjunction with the quality of their research, as determined by our interagency partners, DOE National Laboratory scientists, and our Nuclear Forensics Science Panel. We also perform annual assessments to monitor how well the National Nuclear Forensics Expertise Development Program is meeting the demands of the nuclear forensics workforce.

Question 4. What is DNDO doing to partner with foreign ports to reach the goal of 100% scanning of in-bound cargo? How does DNDO coordinate their efforts with DOE and DOS?

Answer. DNDO's role in the matter of 100% scanning of in-bound cargo is predominantly focused on supporting the technology used in detection and in mission analysis. We develop, acquire, and support the detection systems that could be used by our operational partners for this mandate and we assess risk reduction across the global nuclear detection architecture.

We first conduct research and development on technologies that may be applied to meet the 100% scanning mandate. We are in the process of characterizing the effectiveness and maturity of three different systems that have some ability to detect shielded and unshielded nuclear and other radioactive materials in containerized cargo.

In addition, DNDO collaborates with DOE's Second Line of Defense Program on requirements development, acquisition strategies, technological advancements, capability improvement, and post-deployment lessons learned and data analysis. DNDO has also transferred radiation detectors to DOE for use at foreign ports.

Recently, DHS DNDO teamed with DHS Science and Technology Directorate, Borders and Maritime Security Division to develop a revolutionary high-energy, non-intrusive inspection (NII) system. This system will not only image and support interdiction of shielded and unshielded special nuclear material but will support detection of contraband materials such as explosives, drugs, weapons, currency, and bootleg alcohol and tobacco. Previously, this has required two distinctly different NII systems focused on different threats. This integrated NII system will be installed at a Boston area Massachusetts Port Authority (MASSPORT) facility where it will be jointly tested by DHS, MASSPORT, and the UK Home Office, which is also a partner in this project and looking for an integrated solution.

Question 5. Do you feel that the Memorandum of Understanding between DNDO, NNSA, DTRA, and DNI is sufficient for achieving maximum efficiency in exchanging information between agencies on radiological and nuclear threats?

Answer. Yes. The MOU between DNDO and the National Nuclear Security Administration (NNSA), the Defense Threat Reduction Agency (DTRA), and the Office of the Director of National Intelligence (ODNI) is a very effective means to coordinate research and development efforts related to nuclear detection. The MOU allows full and open access among the parties to on-going research and development, facilitates interagency representation in program reviews and proposal evaluations, and affords easy access to R&D findings, thereby increasing efficiency and reducing duplication of effort. The Nuclear Defense Research and Development Roadmap, Fiscal Years 2013–2017, developed by the interagency through the National Science and Technology Council's Committee on Homeland and National Security, enables further coordination and information exchange across the interagency.

DNDO also works closely with DTRA, NNSA, and ODNI to share information on radiological and nuclear threats. As part of our risk analysis process, interagency experts, including those at DHS/I&A, are surveyed on the likelihood of different threat scenarios. DNDO collaborates closely with NNSA to estimate the theoretical capabilities of different adversaries to develop improvised nuclear devices. This information is then used to support, develop, and maintain the global nuclear detection architecture and related efforts.

Question 6. The NSC has established coordination mechanisms, including a Countering Nuclear Threats Interagency Policy Committee, for international nuclear and radiological border security efforts. Do you feel that this has significantly improved interagency cooperation for nuclear smuggling? If not, how could the coordination be maximized?

Answer. Engagement with staff from the National Security Council is beneficial and improves coordination efforts by providing a high-level venue to gain interagency concurrence and address concerns. Indeed, DNDO was created through the interagency process and remains committed to working with the National Security Council to continue to strengthen interagency coordination. For example, the 2010 and 2014 Global Nuclear Detection Architecture Strategic Plans and the 2010 National Strategic Five-Year Plan for Improving the Nuclear Forensics and Attribution Capabilities of the United States were vetted and approved utilizing the same process. Coupled with other, non-White House-led mechanisms, such as the Global Nuclear Detection Architecture Interagency Working Group, the Nuclear Forensics Executive Council, and the National Technical Nuclear Forensics Steering Committee, coordination efforts continue to improve to ensure a holistic and efficient interagency approach to detecting nuclear and other radioactive materials out of regulatory control.

Question 7a. DNDO is participating in the European Union initiated Illicit Trafficking Radiological Assessment Program, or ITRAP+10, so-called because they are revisiting the original assessment 10 years later. This program involved testing of numerous types of radiation detection equipment including RPMs.

Specifically what is DNDO's involvement in that program?

Question 7b. How is DNDO using the results of this testing in making decisions to procure new RPMs or other radiation detection equipment?

Answer. The ITRAP+10 program was a true partnership for us with the European Commission's Joint Research Center. Both parties contributed funding, facilities, scientists, test personnel, and radiological and nuclear sources to execute this program. ITRAP+10 also included sharing of scientific subject-matter experts for peer review, joint test and analysis plans, and sharing of specialized test equipment to ensure consistent results. In all, ITRAP+10 tested 79 commercially-available models in nine categories of instruments against standards accepted by the American National Standards Institute and the International Electrotechnical Commission.

Specifically, DNDO:

- Tested 47 models of instruments to the full complement of consensus standards, which included testing to extreme environmental, mechanical, and electro-magnetic influences,
- Developed novel instrumentation and standardized source kits and test phantoms,
- Will publish 47 individual vendor reports detailing the performance against standards of each of instrument tested,
- Will publish nine comprehensive reports with the JRC which will survey the status of current generation detectors, and
- Will archive the complete data set for future use.

Results from the ITRAP+10 efforts have directly supported two acquisition programs for the Department and numerous requests from other Federal, State, and local officials. For example, the Small Vessel Stand-Off Detection program has used the data from the testing to inform performance and operational testing, and the Human Portable Tripwire program was able to leverage the ITRAP+10 spectroscopic radiation personal detector tests to revise quantitative requirements at substantial savings.

ITRAP+10 results are also being used to inform the Analysis of Alternatives for the Radiation Portal Monitor Program.

○

www.ingramcontent.com/pod-product-compliance
Lightning Source LLC
Chambersburg PA
CBHW080623290526

45790CB00007B/2898